The Man in the Black Hat

Collected Columns from the *Chatham Courier*

Albert S. Callan

HOLLIS
PUBLISHING

ISBN 1-884186-26-2

Printed in the United States of America.

Hollis Publishing Company
95 Runnells Bridge Road, Hollis, NH 03049
(t) 603.889.4500   (f) 603.889.6551
books@hollispublishing.com

Contents

Introduction . . . .*v*

Prologue . . . .*vii*

Main Street 1

School Days 35

History Notes 49

Country Life 83

Postcards to Chatham 125

At the Table 159

Bright Lights 189

Celebrations 217

For my bride, Virginia,
whose love, support and encouragement made this work possible

A.S.C.

INTRODUCTION

When a group of regular readers of Albert Callan's weekly column "The Man in The Black Hat" first broached the idea of collecting a selection of those columns into a book, we instinctively sought to measure the scope of his work in familiar, tangible units of time and space: years, seasons, lines, words. The more columns we read, however, the more we came to see that what most commended them to being collected and passed on to future generations of readers was not their statistically impressive span across decades, or the hundreds of linear inches of column space they represented. It was rather the timelessness of the unhurried observations they contained of human nature and the human condition, steeped in the rolling hills and shady back roads of Columbia County, New York.

Albert is a master at teaching the enduring virtues and verities of a reflective life, because he has learned them so well himself that they inform and illuminate all of his writing, whatever the subject and from wherever he writes. Many of the stories of people and events that unfold in these pages belong to a simpler, less agitated time, and yet the more recent columns lead us there too, because of the gloriously old-fashioned qualities they celebrate. In the world of which Albert writes, nothing is hurried, whether it be a train making its way to Chatham from Manhattan, bread rising, or snow melting. He clarifies the essence of life, and extends that gift to all his readers, even those who have never been in his beloved Hudson

Valley. In letting us forget for a moment the dizzying speed which has become the hallmark of so many aspects of twenty-first-century life, he reminds us that it is the regretful burden of every generation to know that they once lived slower lives, in simpler times.

And so memory is often the currency with which Albert barters for his next column. There are columns which delight in the past while acknowledging, at times regretfully, that seasons change, children grow up, shops close forever and Thanksgiving leftovers get stale. Some are simple exercises in the art of finding solace in the beauty of a countryside unchanged for centuries, road maps to a landscape whose sights and smells, boundaries and treelines have been etched in the writer's heart since childhood. Others are wry explications of otherwise unfathomable country rituals, or reminders to look up when passing a certain bend in the road because the view just there is, well, just so. In the truest tradition of both the poet and the philosopher (and Albert is a bit of both), topics both large and small are carefully held up to his lamp, from the laying of a single egg to the end of WWII.

We are grateful to Albert for helping us understand and appreciate that which surrounds us, be it a mountain, a hill, an animal, or one of our fellows. We may or may not pass by the fields and roads of which he writes, but we will all recognize in the journey the evocation of a time and place that reaches beyond mere words and says, stop, this is home.

Friends of "The Black Hat"

Prologue

We can do the math together—one column a week, times 52 weeks a year, times 56 years, gives us 2,912 written by yours truly since that fateful day in 1947 when this space crept into the *Chatham Courier*. At an average of 1,200 words per column, that's about 3,454,400 words.

Have I ever written the same column twice? Probably, but not intentionally. Going through dusty clippings I've found half-a-dozen almost point-for-point offerings written several years apart, but then, some stories are worth repeating.

Over the years, the questions most frequently asked of me are (1) "How and why did you start to write the column?" and (2) "How did it get the name 'The Man in the Black Hat'?"

The *Courier* always had gossipy tidbits going back to the 19th century. For example, this item is from the February 12, 1887, edition: "A certain Spencertown lady had better close her blinds lest she blind half the swain in that community who amuse themselves these cold winter nights peeping in her bedroom."

In 1946, when I returned from World War II and became editor, the thought came to mind, all the good guys in the movies wear white hats; the bad ones wear black. Why not write a column called "The Man in the Black Hat"? Thus cloaked in anonymity, I could search out all the juicy tidbits of scandal that only a villainous person would report. "The Hat" enjoyed immediate popularity as I frequented local watering holes that yielded a wealth of innuendo for early columns.

In the late 1940s, the column gained nationwide notoriety when the largest floating crap game east of the Mississippi moved into the city of Hudson. Shortly thereafter, "The Hat" began weekly reports on the dice derby's operations, not a full column but invasive details on the big-time rollers and nightly takes which, on weekends, exceeded $250,000. The *Courier* was the only newspaper reporting the gaming room operations, and a vice lord offered us $2,000 to "forget what was happening in Hudson." We didn't. The superintendent of the state police paid us a visit, asking if we could verify our allegations. Of course we could, and a few days later troopers raided Hudson's brothels, but someone had tipped the games and only empty tables were found in the old Diamond Street building which housed the games of chance.

An investigation followed, lasting two years, but indictments were as rare as four aces, and the probe fizzled out.

In 1950, the *Courier* and the column were nominated for a Pulitzer Prize for "Best Community Reporting," only to be edged out by the *San Francisco Chronicle,* which had had a reporter killed covering a tong war in that city. The question remains: If I had been rubbed out, would the *Courier* have won a Pulitzer in absentia of "The Hat"?

I am proud that I have never missed a deadline; no mean trick as we spend winters in Mexico and are subject to the erratic whims of that nation's electronic systems. In closing, may I thank my readers who have made this a most amusing job. For all the supportive notes I've received, all the closely reasoned arguments sometimes filled with rage, all the gestures of affection; thank you for showing up. I'll try to keep doing the same.

—*Albert S. Callan*

MAIN STREET

What Was Chatham Like Back in 1862?

As a native of Chatham approaching four score years, I am looked upon as a bit of an oddity by city dwellers who spend their summers in Columbia County. At the same time, I find our city cousins extremely interested in the history of Chatham village and as a former village historian, I am always happy to share my knowledge of community chronicles with them.

Let's for a moment then step back 131 years to what was then known as Chatham Four Corners when the *Chatham Courier* first went to press in a dark little barn on Kinderhook Street.

The name *four corners* denoted the juncture of what is now Route 66 (Main Street), Center Street, River Street and the extension of Austerlitz Street.

Chatham has grown from a few clustered buildings, gathered about a nucleus of roads, to its present modernism. If you lived in Chatham Four Corners in 1862, Kinderhook Street, as it is now known, was little more than a good country road with the vast Starks' family farmland and buildings that made up the extreme western end. Other than the buildings that made up this estate, there were but five or six residences, the greater number of which lined the south side of the street. It was down this thoroughfare that former President Martin Van Buren rode on his favorite horse en route to Peter Groat's tavern, the present 1811 Inn. The former chief executive would enjoy a glass of wine, perhaps take a light collation, chat with Mr. Groat about affairs of the day, then mount his steed and return to Kinderhook.

The business section of Chatham Four Corners was composed of approximately 15 retail establishments. Early village records indicate that there about four grocery stores in 1863—perhaps not grocery stores as we think of them today, but they were emporiums that were stocked to fill the needs of villagers and nearby farmers. They probably would best be described in today's world as "country stores."

John and Jim Traver conducted their business on Main Street at the site of the former B. H. Delson store. The Burrows' store stood on Park Row on what is today a vacant lot where once stood the New York State Electric and Gas building. Jerry Best operated on Main Street next to the Travers and the fourth store was owned by Homer Crandell on the site of the present Fleet Bank building. A dry goods and notions store could be found on upper Hudson Ave., where Video Visions is found today. A five and dime store owned by the Griswold brothers did business on the present site of the Gentlemen and Ladies Shoppe on Park Row.

Matt and Joe Lord operated an exclusive oyster shop where the Chatham Laundromat now stands. Barrels of iced oysters from the Boston market arrived daily on the Boston and Albany Railroad. The *Courier* advised its readers, "There's nothing better than to have a dozen Cape Cod oysters served up by the Lord brothers." Price 20 cents. Oysters were the only commodity sold on these premises, packed in kegs and sold from a dozen to a keg full. The conservative buyer was obliged to furnish his or her own receptacle; the now familiar pint-sized cardboard carton with the wire handles was yet a future invention.

The present location of Lanphear's Service Center was then the corner of Park Row and Main Street. Here was the drugstore of Jacob L. Best. Where the Brown Shoe Company stands today, Milton Ford conducted the village's only haberdashery and exhibited the latest styles for the smartly dressed man.

Probably the principal industry of any size in the community was a combination blast furnace, foundry and machine shop operated in a structure that extended from the present town clock building to the Chatham Bookstore. The chief products manufactured here were tread mills known locally as "Horse Powers." It was in the blast furnace that the catastrophic fire of 1869 started and swept up the east side of Main Street. Ocean Fire Co. No. 1 responded to the conflagration but the flames were so intense and spreading so quickly that firemen from Rensselaer and Hudson brought their apparatus by trains to help fight the blaze. The fire was finally halted when firemen dynamited a small building that stood on the site of the present Mini-Chopper parking lot. This created a fire break and halted the flames before they spread to the Chatham Reformed Church, where Keith G. Flint, Esq., conducts his law practice today.

Perhaps as interesting as any account of the early village was the introduction of electric lighting. We are told that some 20 oil street lamps were cleaned and lighted each afternoon. They burned about a pint of oil during the hours of darkness. They were allowed to burn out in the early morning hours and filled again when relighted. It was about 110 years ago that the late John Klinglesmith, former Chatham justice of the peace, with James Morehouse formed the first Chatham Electric Light Company. The Steinkill Creek furnished water power just east of Center Street where the New York State Electric & Gas Co. power station was located for many years.

Only the more courageous or wealthy ventured to try the new lighting system in their homes, and stores were slow to adopt its use. There was a five-year interlude before the community fathers approved its use for street lighting.

The first amusement or opera house was Cady's Hall, on Main Street, where The Firm now holds forth, and it was here that traveling minstrel and stage shows paid periodic visits.

In the latter days of the 19th century, Cady's Hall became known far and wide for the long-distance running races staged within its confines. Contestants would come from all parts of the Northeast and would race around the hall each evening over a period of up to five days. Each runner had a trainer who would pass him a beverage or nourishment and then collect the bottles or plates a few laps later.

The tale is told that the finest runner in these parts came from Kinderhook and a large crowd of his hometown fans filled the hall to cheer him on to victory. The Kinderhooker, according to legend, was leading in the final stretch when his running pants suddenly fell down over his feet. He tripped and sprawled on the track a few feet from the finish line, allowing a fleet-footed Philmont farmer to take first place. As for the Kinderhook runner, he was disqualified by the judges because his trainer had no blanket to cover his nudity.

So, back in those days, Chatham Four Corners was living, romancing, progressing and struggling toward becoming a greater and better place to live. The efforts of our predecessors have been far from in vain. Late in the 19th century a Chatham Board of Trades was formed and they sent posters with railroad men on the Harlem Division to be put up in Grand Central Station and nearby hotels. The posters proclaimed:

COME TO CHATHAM!
- Chatham offers opportunities for a home away from the grime and confusion of the city.
- Chatham has all the comforts and none of the perplexities of cosmopolitan life.
- Chatham's air is wholesome; its hills are virgin; its scenery is sublime.

- Chatham is a God-fearing Sunday-observing, moral-loving, right-preaching and right-practicing community.
- Chatham's homes are mannered with an hospitable people whose interests do not seem to be confined to four walls and a family tree.
- Chatham's stores meet all the requirements of any reasonable existence.
- Chatham, professionally, is ably fortified. Her doctors of medicine are second to none. Her doctors of law are without peer. Her doctors of divinity will take front rank anywhere.
- Chatham, geographically, is the center of it. She has wealth on the South; eructation on the East; relaxation on the North; exhilaration on the West. Chatham is a good place to live!

⟫⋄⟪

Hudson's Bodies Beautiful
Holbrook Co., Coachmakers Supreme to Early Auto Trade,
Flourished Briefly in the 1920s

During the coming spring and summer months, the raucous bleating of klaxons will announce the gathering of antique cars owned by collectors of these vintage vehicles. The Automobilists of the Upper Hudson Valley frequently schedule meets in and around Columbia County, and last year the Veteran Motor Car Club of America conducted a tour that brought a convoy of shining cars, with forgotten names, chugging along Route 22 and over into the Berkshires.

Today's generations probably will not recognize the nameplates on the cars which provided favored transportation in the roaring

20s. Fortunate indeed is the antique-automobile buff who operated a Mercer, Fox, Lafayette, Reo, Stutz Bearcat; and extremely lucky is the owner with an additional plaque on his vehicle carrying the legend "Holbrook Auto Body Co. Hudson, N.Y."

Fond recollections of the Holbrook Company were recalled in a recent issue of *True* magazine which published a "Famous Automobile Portrait" by artist Melbourne Brindle. The subject of his colors was a rare $33,000 Crane Simplex which had been designed for exhibit at the San Francisco Auto Salon in 1916. Often called the "American Mercedes," so famous was its excellence, this particular showpiece chariot has a marine motif throughout. The yacht-like body was put on by the Holbrook Company, including two fresh-air intakes in its cowl made to resemble a ship's ventilator; two portholes are below. No front doors mar the lines of the "hull"; entry is from the rear via a "walk through deck." Two spare wheels aft are locked by a large brass propeller. What made this strange amphibian go? Four wheels and a ponderous six-cylinder engine delivered 70 knots in a favorable wind. This particular Hudson-built car was owned for many years by the artist Mr. Brindle, who later sold it to the owner of a club in Reno, Nevada, where it is currently on exhibit.

The Crane Simplex was one of many creations turned out at an enormous cost by the Columbia County Coachmakers. One of those who best remembers Holbrook's operations is Deno Gazzera, 71-year-old Hudson resident, who was one of Holbrook's experts in shaping fenders. He had learned the art of molding metal in his native Italy, and his wife even earned more money than he did at Holbrook as a welder. Mr. Gazzera recalls that the Holbrook Company first operated on West End Ave. and 62nd St. in New York City about 1909. Gradually, the plant's production increased and it outgrew its Manhattan accommodations. Taxes also went up proportionately, so in 1920, Holbrook moved its staff up to Hudson and occupied the site of the present Universal Match Co. on Route 66 in Greenport.

No modern-day assembly line greeted the visitor to the Holbrook plant. More than 350 men and some women worked seven days a week creating for individual owners a racy Stearns roadster or a sleek Rolls-Royce cabriolet.

Holbrook's largest customer was the Packard Motor Car Company which sent a simple chassis frame and motor to Hudson. From this meager beginning, the artisans molded fenders and installed hand-wrought dashboards, while in another department real leather seats were carefully sewn in the open Packard touring cars. The metal shop echoed to the throb of hundreds of hammers as the Packard shells were hand-shaped from strips of aluminum. There followed an application of paint that probably never has been matched in today's modern body-building methods.

After a coat of primer was applied by hand, five coats of "rough stuff" base paint in the car vernacular were brushed on the body. The shell then stood three days to allow the paint to dry and then it was sanded by hand to remove any dimples or rough spots. The favorite Packard colors in those days were green and maroon and they were applied by skilled artists. Three coats of color were carefully painted on, with a thorough rubbing between each application to ensure smoothness. Then two coats of varnish, followed by more rubbing, before a final coat of clear varnish which made the Packard a thing of beauty. The drying process took three weeks before the automobiles were ready to leave the line and head back for show rooms in Manhattan.

Each year the Holbrook Company turned out some 600 cars, not only Packards but Mercedes, Fiats and Stearns. Almost every car carried a price tag of $9,000 and up, depending on the owner's desire for special handicraft. On special occasions, a Rolls-Royce chassis would roll into the Hudson shop. The shell of this car was completed by Holbrook but the icing on the cake was applied at a plant in Springfield, Mass., where the vehicle's many special instruments were installed.

The Holbrook Company thrived from 1920 through 1924, but then a fellow named Henry Ford brought out a tin lizzie called the Model T and suddenly the American public found that almost every family could enjoy the luxury of a car, and at a nominal cost. Assembly lines appeared throughout the nation and spelled doom for the coachmakers who toiled by hand. In 1935, after an unsuccessful stock issue to bolster the company's finances, the Holbrook Company realized it could not meet the competition of automation in its infancy and closed the doors of its Hudson plant.

Hundreds of men were left jobless, but 1925 was a good year; the Depression was still four years away, so many found work in other plants. A few, however, still had work in custom body building, only this time they were repairing cars wrecked on the highways. Today Holbrook is remembered by another generation, but youngsters who smash up a sports car can bring it to Deno's Auto Body Shop on Hudson's 6th Street, where Deno Gazzera will carefully rap out the dents using much the same technique he employed 50 years ago when he turned out the finest Packard touring cars in the nation—just ask the man who owned one!

⇒·◇·⇐

The Very Best and the Worst Chatham Fairs

That brief period of time we call summer, roughly between Memorial Day and Labor Day, speeds by faster with each passing year.

Nope, they don't make years like they used to. This one, which began with a New Year's hangover only a few days ago, is already on the other side of the mountain and going fast. April was perky. June rhymes with moon, but August sounds absolutely exhausted, like the New York Mets.

There are lots of things to worry about in August, as summer fades like the tan you were supposed to get on those sun-filled (hot!) July afternoons. Meanwhile, here in Columbia County, we are about to welcome September, which means (all together now!) the BIG Chatham Fair, the annual bucolic extravaganza that helps us into autumn and eventually into the icy grip of King Winter.

The fair always brings out the boy-who-loves-the-fair in me. As I've done for more years than I can remember, I've toured the fairgrounds almost daily to watch the metamorphosis from empty buildings to the Labor Day weekend extravaganza filled with sights, sounds and smells that spell the Chatham Fair.

In my four score and four years of life, I can happily recall some of the more exciting fairs that graced the old grounds. Perhaps the first was in 1923, when it was announced that an aeroplane (sic) would land at the fairgrounds and take passengers aloft. It didn't seem possible that a flying machine could land and take off on the track infield. On the appointed day, however, a large biplane glided down and people lined up to soar over the countryside. All went well until late in the first afternoon, when the pilot didn't see a large hole in the field and lost a wheel. The plane remained an oddity for several days until it was loaded on a rail flatcar and unceremoniously left Chatham.

That same year, the Labor Day feature was a sham battle in which National Guard infantrymen, some playing good American soldiers, some portraying the "enemy," charged back and forth across the infield firing rifles and machine guns. A packed grandstand stood and cheered (I along with them) as the American dough-boys drove the infidels into Gray Swamp adjacent to the grounds and the Ghent Band played the National Anthem.

After the troops departed, every kid in Chatham swarmed onto the "battlefield" to collect spent cartridge casings by the thousands. Fourteen years later, when I was assistant manager of the Chatham High baseball squad, while raking the infield, what did I find? Cartridge casings.

It was in 1932 that a horrendous infantile paralysis epidemic swept the nation and medical experts warned to keep children away from crowds lest they fall victims to the disease. Seemingly no parents in Chatham acknowledged this warning and all my friends attended the fair. But my father and mother decided it was best to stay home and that was akin to a death sentence. To sit in my Payn Avenue home in the evening and see the fairgrounds' lights, hear the merry-go-round's music and the barkers' spiels made it the WORST fair in my memory. By the way, 10 days later I was diagnosed with polio.

The 1940 Centennial Fair stands out in my memory as that was the first year I became truly active in a fair event. Clifford Hodge, a fair director and the *Chatham Courier*'s editor, said the fair was looking for someone to head up an antique car show, would I do it? Sure! With the late Elizabeth Crandell, whose father was a fair board member, we combed the county and adjacent states for antique vehicles. It was amazing what turned up in old barns—cars dating back to the early 1900s, and many in mint condition. James Melton, the New York Opera star and car buff, came to judge the entries and went home with a Stutz Bearcat.

A historical pageant was staged that year highlighting important events in the county's history. One was the arrival of Henry Hudson and his welcome by the Indians. We performed on the track before the grandstand emitting guttural Indian grunts and doing a shuffling Indian dance. Our bodies had been lathered with a dark red liquid to give us a true ethnic coloring. Hudson came forth to greet us and at that moment it began raining in torrents. Instantly, his redskinned friends became white teenagers. But the show must go on, and we greeted Henry warmly despite the change in coloration. The rain stopped and we bashfully retired to our teepees.

It was in 1946 that I was selected to the fair's board of managers. The late Ralph O. Hoffman had been named the previous year and we were the "kids" among a distinguished panel of elderly county residents. We met at the White Mills home of the fair's secretary, William A. Dardess. The fair was badly in debt in those days and every conceivable way to save money was foremost on the agenda. I remember one night the issue was: Should the fair hire a popular black Chathamite to be custodian of the men's toilet or should they obtain the services of a prominent Hudson African American to do the job?

After endless debate, it was decided to hire the Hudsonian as he might bring more friends with him on the "Fair Special" train from Hudson than the Chatham gentleman could produce. At the end of each evening, Mr. Dardess' daughter, Mary E. Dardess of Chatham scholastic fame, would serve coffee and sandwiches. The evenings were as quiet and unexciting as the fair of those days.

Until just before World War II, the fair ran for a full week and featured vaudeville shows every day. In all my years, the best act ever staged was Norbu the Gorilla. There's this guy dressed up in a gorilla suit and he's dragged out on stage in a heavy cage. A scantily clad young thing, a lithesome blonde, enters the cage and waves a whip at the ape. With that, Norbu breaks down the cage door, leaps down on the track and heads for the grandstand. Norbu was a sensational gymnast and in seconds scaled the grandstand columns, slithered down and headed into the crowd. Never have you seen so many people scattered in different directions. We best recall two small towheaded boys (now approaching 50) springing out of the grandstand and sprinting up the midway. I suppose Norbu has gone to that great jungle in the sky by now, but he'll always be my favorite act.

And let's not forget Adele Nelson's elephants. Adele resided just outside of Ghent and toured the nation with her elephant act. When not on the road, she tethered her pachyderms in her farm fields and let them forage. The story is told of some city hunters who came stealing silently out of the woods only to be confronted by five enormous elephants. It's said they threw down their weapons, ran as fast as they could to their car and disappeared in a cloud of dust, never to return again.

⟹•⟸

Kinderhook Creek Waters Brought Early Prosperity to Rider's Mills

Early in the 18th century Malden Bridge was settled by a family named Mosher. They established on the Kinderhook Creek, near the now demolished Peaslee Mill, a paper pulp mill. Thus, the first name was Mosher Mills. Soon after this the Rider family migrated here from Connecticut, purchased the mill and a large tract of land and the name was changed to Rider's Mills. One of the first projects of construction was a covered bridge which spanned the Kinderhook Creek below the bend, guarded by gigantic elm trees at either end. This was a necessity, providing a crossing at this point. The Kinderhook is a mighty stream in flood times and had a "keen appetite" for that bridge. In the flood of 1866, the original span was swept downstream. It was carried along with a grist mill, saw mill and a large dam above the bridge.

At this period Rider's Mills had flourished. In 1815 Horace W. Peaslee had come from the Connecticut Valley along with others seeking to better themselves. Reaching this locality, as a paper maker by trade, he readily visualized the possibilities the waters of the Kinderhook would offer a paper mill. He operated the pulp mill until 1835, when he erected the larger paper mill on the opposite side near the present bridge. He installed machinery to manufacture straw paper. These were the largest mills of their kind for many miles. They operated 24 hours a day, from 1835 to 1898, changing shifts at 12 midnight and working by candlelight. Unusual for that period, many women were employed. They turned out first-class paper with their watermark—long since forgotten. The locality prospered with added employment and a market for the farmers' straw. Also men were sought, as good teamsters to drive many yokes of Peaslee oxen used to haul the paper to Stockbridge, Mass., where it was shipped by rail or downriver from Albany, to a ready market that was waiting in New York. The ox carts that went to Stockbridge did not return empty. They carted lime from the pits they used in the manufacture of paper. This necessitated not only drivers but a blacksmith shop to shoe the oxen, horses and mules.

In a small, white cottage near the bridge lived the village smithy, one John Holt, Sr., who shod the four-footed beasts for fifty-five years. He was assisted by one Thomas Cornell, a veteran of the Civil War who had traveled much and was not loathe to tell of his adventures. In addition to the Peaslee Mill, the village boasted 14 houses, a shoemaker, wagon maker, cheese factory (the latter was moved to Chatham Center for a freight house), grist mill and grocery, meat market, and the blacksmith shop. The old pulp mill had long since been demolished.

This was a progressive community, which was proved by the construction of one of the earliest schools in New York State, about 1780. It was constructed of native brick from a clay pit near Old Chatham. The early settlers donated their labor and carted the brick to the school site. Built with a massive front door, District No. 3, the "Brick Schoolhouse," stands sturdily today.

The original bridge was replaced in 1866 by another that was carried downstream a quarter of a mile in a flood in 1869. It was towed back the following summer and elevated two feet. This bridge staunchly defied floods, including the flood of 1938 when it was half submerged in water. Badly damaged, it was repaired. Covered bridges were not only picturesque but most practical. The upkeep was more than one-third as economical as an ordinary "plank one." The only drawback was in winter when sleighs were used with heavy loads; they had to first "snow," or shovel snow, for the sleigh runners to glide on. In the flood of 1948, the covered bridge was swept downstream and broken into bits. A new, modern bridge was built higher to span the creek.

The Peaslee Mill hit its peak of production during the Civil War. With demands for more paper, all help available was eagerly sought. During this time Horace Peaslee married Ann Carpenter of Brainard, N.Y. One of Mrs. Peaslee's stories she often narrated of her girlhood occurred when she was 14 years of age. Word had spread of the tour of Marquis de Lafayette and son and that an escort of Gen. Solomon Van Rensselaer, Col. Clinton, Col. Cooper, Major Van Schaak and officers of Col. Cooper's Dragoons would pass through en route to Columbia Hall at Lebanon Springs. Garlands of flowers were hung and baskets of flowers waiting. Riding in a two-wheeled rig, the Marquis and his son passed directly beneath Carpenter's verandah. Ann threw a rose which landed in the Marquis' lap. He acknowledged the favor and blew her a kiss.

The Peaslees enjoyed their prosperity, owning large properties and many fine horses. The famous "Antinore" stallion was raised by Horace Peaslee on one of his farms. The estate of the late W. Gordon Cox is still known as Antinore Farm. In the spring floods of 1885, Mr. Peaslee, as was his usual custom, went out for a smoke and a walk over the bridge to the mill. He never returned. He fell off the bridge and was found the next morning drowned in the Kinderhook—the waters which had given him wealth.

⋙⋆⋘

The Courier *Marks 130th Anniversary*

Well, bless my soul, it's October 1992 and the year is rapidly drawing to a close, but before it does, may we lift a glass to the *Courier* on the occasion of its 130th birthday. It was in 1862 that Delos Sutherland, a man of considerable literary and poetic talent, came over from South Adams, Mass., and set up a print shop for posterity with a historical marker. The paper was four pages, issued every Thursday, with a subscription of one dollar, "payable in advance." When the publication made its debut, the *Albany Argus* noted that it was "executed with neatness, accuracy and dispatch." Conservative in its editorial views, the *Courier* was the official county newspaper for the Republican Party for more than a century. In fact, for many years, no one knew who the Democratic candidates were because the *Courier* never put their names in print. What was Chatham like 130 years ago?

Well, let's take a look at an October 1862 issue, which we have treasured through the years.

Let's see, here's a wedding notice that Mr. E. C. Tripp and Miss Fanny Peake were married, and the editor observed, "a liberal fee accompanied this notice and we make special acknowledgment. The Twains have our best wishes." . . . "William Peake of Chatham was undergoing the Water Cure at Saratoga Springs at the time of a fire Sunday and lit everything but the clothes on his back" . . . Excitement reigned in the village when posters went up announcing the appearance of "Ball's Great American Collosseum [sic] featuring Antique Olympic Games, Grotesque Dances, Classic Posturing, Comic Scenes, Pantomimes and Ethiopian Comedians." . . . The issue was filled with advertisements for medical tonics, including "Dr. Chessman's Female Pills, Dr. Wishart's Pine Tree Cordial—the best remedy for throat and lung diseases—" and if you were real racy you might have purchased a copy of "Dr. La Croix Private Medical Treatise on the Psychological Views of Marriage." . . . Among the latter-day Dr. Kinsey's writings were "Confessions of Thrilling Interest of a Boarding School Miss, A College Student and a Married Lady" . . . A. Hoes offered "first class rum and cheroots" at the Chatham House and Dr. F. Maxon advertised himself as "The French Physician and Surgeon." It was noted that the good doctor "has a rare faculty of telling patients their complaints at once, without any information from them and will prescribe effectual remedies of all curable cases, or, if the patient is beyond relief, he will tell them so."

Oliver Folette of Pittsfield must have blushed a bit when he entered this ad: "LOST in the vicinity of Stanwix Hall tavern on Saturday night, a small, green Brussels carpet bag. A $5 reward will be paid by the subscriber" . . . For those about to depart this life, Hiram B. Mather of Spencertown, the local undertaker, offered a "Splendid City Hearse" for a final ride to the cemetery . . . Editor Sutherland voiced this familiar complaint: "These are fine days for printers; job printing is now taxed five percent, advertisements three percent and ordinary printing paper is 24 cents a pound. Something has to be done with those people down in Washington to reduce taxes and help the small businessman." . . . In a column of local news, one item is headed: WHERE'S BARNUM? "There is a lady living in Chatham over 70 years old who has never seen a railroad locomotive, a telegraph, a steamboat or a printing press." . . . And this titillating article from the New Lebanon correspondent: "A West Street lady whose name we won't mention for fear she might be someone's grandma has been arrested for confessing to affairs with a Pittsfield gentleman long before her marriage and continuing until discovery by her husband a few days since!"

Farmers were offered this bit of advice to prevent cattle from jumping fences: "Clip off the eyelashes of the underlids with a pair of scissors, whereby the ability or disposition to jump is effectively destroyed as Sampson's power was by the loss of his locks." . . . And there was the headline A LOYAL WOMAN: "There's a woman residing in Hudson, Mrs. B., who has been married no less than four times. All her liege lords have been soldiers. Her last husband was killed a few days ago and rumor has it that she's about to do it again for her country." . . . Under the Federal Stores (Old Chatham) column was this note directed at "Mr. J," which said, "Since we have seen you on several occasions trying to convince your shadow that it's improper to follow a gentleman, we think its high time you stayed out of the local tavern and joined a temperance society."

Chatham maidens were in a "high state" as "quite a number of soldiers in the 1st N.Y. Mounted Rifles were home on furlough and took them to the White Mills Sabbath School picnic. A good time is reported." . . . Best-seller of the day: Beadle's Dime Novel, "The Moosehunter—highly entertaining" . . . A tinge of sadness was noted regarding the Albany weekly *Knickerbocker,* which had suspended publication. Reason: "high price of paper, material and labor." . . . A contest was held at Coburn's Hall to find the "homeliest old bachelor, the homeliest married man, handsomest married man, homeliest old maid and the lady and gentleman with the strongest lungs as tested by the Spriometer." . . . Also, "The New York gentleman who bargained for the Stanwix Hall on Central Square in Chatham has backed out. Mr. Bain will continue to conduct the establishment. He knows how to keep a good hotel. Long may he wave!"

From Claverack came the sobering report that a young woman had shot herself through the heart. "She was only 18 and married, but her husband, having enlisted in the Army and failed to correspond with her, she took up with another, became remorseful and put an end to her existence." . . . Chatham was both amused and puzzled by "The Wandering Poet," as he styled himself, "who came into town on the afternoon Rutland train and exhibited to a crowd at the Kinderhook Street station the facility with which he could make rhymes on any given subject. He wasn't to be sneezed at." . . . An editorial cast shame on the community of Coeymans, "where a party of 20 young men departed a few days ago for Canada to escape the draft." . . . A Kinderhook attorney, "the only one in the village who is habitually given to fibbing, informs us a child was born in that place a few days since, that, in less than an hour after its birth, rubbed its eyes and cried out, 'don't put my name in the papers' and then expired. Wonderful place, Kinderhook." . . . And here's a Madison Avenue approach to advertising: "The entrance to a woman's heart is through her eye or ear, but a philosopher has said the way to a man's heart is down his throat. Good housewives understand this and use Herrick Allen's Gold Medal Saleratus."

Best story of the issue came from over in Punsit Valley . . . "A person appearing to be about 16 years old, and professing to be an orphan named Henry I. Goodwin, who was attempting to get money to go to college, obtained work at the Mather farm. Friday he was taken ill and asked that a bowl of gruel be brought to him while in bed. A physician was called and pronounced the case hopeless, but while the person was insensible, the physician made an examination and discovered the patient was a woman! A fine bowie knife was found among her effects, doubtless intended for defense against insult."—in Spencertown?

—————◆—————

The Erastus Corning Story
Crippled Boy, 11, Left New Concord to Become Millionaire President of the New York Central

On a mild day early in the spring of 1805, a weary family arrived in the little hamlet of New Concord, Columbia County, after traveling from Norwich, Conn., over the Hudson and Eastern Turnpike. The journey had been long and hard and during a greater part of the trek the adults had walked beside their wagon-load of belongings to their new home in New York State. One of the family, however, was unable to walk. Atop the wagon rode a dark-eyed lad of 11 years. His name was Erastus Corning.

The father of this brood, which would eventually number 11, was Bliss Corning, a man who was never a "money maker"; in fact, during most of his years he had been in financial difficulties. In 1807, two years after their arrival in New Concord, the Corning family scraped together the sizable sum of $1,326 to purchase a house and 34 acres of land from Palmer and Rhoda Cady, described in the deed "as situated on the North-side of the road leading from Concord Meeting House to Aaron Cady's." Later, in 1812, Bliss Corning accumulated another $450 and with this money he bought 18 additional acres from the Cady family. Both of these parcels were retained by the father until 1827, when he disposed of them to his son, Erastus, then a resident of Albany, for $1,388.65. At this point, Bliss disappeared, at least so far as his possession of property is concerned, as nothing more regarding him is found in the records of the Columbia County clerk's office.

Young Erastus Corning, however, who had received some education in Connecticut and later at the New Concord school, apparently recognized the very meager circumstances of his father and decided to strike out for himself. So, in 1807, after two years in New Concord, Erastus entered the employ of his uncle, Benjamin Smith, at a hardware store in Troy. It must have been a trying situation for a boy of 13. He had been raised in the country and was acquainted with rural ways. Not only was the city strange to him, but he was hampered physically. As a child of two he had fallen and injured his hip, and now 11 years later he was still forced to use crutches when he walked.

Despite these handicaps, two years later, in 1809, Erastus was in business for himself at the age of 15. He still had an association with his uncle's hardware firm but was now permitted to buy and sell on his own account. Buggy whips apparently were his first venture and, in addition, he bought and sold cigars, pipes, brushes, needles, furs, sugar, lemons and oranges. By 1814, when he was 20, young Corning was rapidly becoming a capitalist, as he was credited then with being worth over $500. The same year he moved to Albany and a year later bought a partnership in John Spencer & Co., a prosperous hardware firm.

Corning was soon to establish himself as one of the outstanding businessmen of Albany and, despite his youth, was recognized as one on whom many honors would be bestowed during his lifetime. In 1819 he married Harriet Weld and, seemingly spurred on by his happy union, he purchased a handsome dwelling at 102 State St. in

Albany, where he lived the remainder of his life. Soon he was to be named an alderman of the city and in 1834 was elected mayor, an office he held until 1837.

Early in life he allied himself with the Democratic Party and as the years rolled on, he played an even more important role in the "Albany Regency," a hard core of devoted Democrats, led by Martin Van Buren of Kinderhook. From 1842 to 1845, Corning was state senator from the Albany District and served two terms in Congress, 1857–59 and 1861–63. During these years his financial interests were expanding. He was buying land in the newly opened west, and investing in banks, including the Hudson River Bank at Hudson. Railroads also occupied his attention and he was largely responsible for the consolidation of several lines with the New York Central. It was not long before Corning became the Central's first president.

It is said that once a person resides in Columbia County he will never be satisfied with any other countryside in the world. The same was true of Erastus Corning. Apparently Columbia's hills made a lasting impression upon him, for in the 1830s, we find him purchasing a house near Canaan, and there he spent several summers with his family. He must have found the former Walker's Store at Canaan a convenient place to do his shopping, for in one of his letters he says he is writing "from the store in the village."

Corning's influence soon spread to other parts of the Empire State. In Steuben County today, there is the City of Corning, noted principally as the site of the Corning Glass Works. The land upon which the present community is located was purchased in 1835 by the Corning Company and the new community was named for the Albany financier. The ability to earn money never left Erastus Corning until his death in 1872, at which time his wealth was estimated at $9 million. A remarkable financial feat for a poor, crippled boy who left New Concord at the age of 13 to enter the business world.

There are still other links between the Corning family and Columbia County.

In the Valatie cemetery, on the south side as one enters the burial ground, stands a 30-foot marble shaft on which is boldly carved the name *Corning*. Beneath this monument rests Bliss Corning, father of Erastus, who died in 1847; his wife, Lucinda, who passed away in 1831; and, John, Hannah and Clarissa. John, the last of the family buried in Valatie, was interred in 1869. Now the question arises, why is it that the family, with the exception of Erastus, was buried in Valatie? According to Miss Louise Hardenbrook, the able Town of Kinderhook historian, Bliss Corning came to live with his daughter, Mrs. Benajah Conant, the former Mary Corning, and probably spent his last days in Valatie. Bliss, however, never had enough money in all his life to erect a monument of such proportions over his grave. Thus is must be assumed that Erastus paid the final honors to his parents, for only a very wealthy man could have afforded such a magnificent stone.

———◆———

GOP Dems

Hey there! Are you one of those dreaded liberal Democrats or an old-fashioned conservative Republican? In less than a week either a liberal or a conservative will be elected President of the United States. Obviously, the thing now is to be conservative. But how can you tell? The fact is that so many people are confused in their own minds what they are. So, dear readers, search yourself fearlessly and take stock, face up to any tinge of liberalism you may have and stamp it out before the word gets around.

Generally speaking, a few simple tests will set you straight. Most important is the Bread Wrapper Test. A Republican always ties the little plastic strip neatly around the bread wrapper, twisting it tightly at least twice. A Democrat, at best, sort of crimps it back on with a half-twist which unwinds and falls off. People you see coming out of white, wooden churches, lighted at night, are Republicans. Democrats buy most of the books that have been banned somewhere. Republicans form censorship committees and read the books as a group. Republicans are likely to have fewer but larger debts that cause them no concern. Democrats consume three-fourths of the rutabaga produced in this country. The rest is thrown out. Democrats never put out ashtrays which have Thank You For Not Smoking printed on the bottom. Republicans will. (Democrats, however, fan the air when you light up and pointedly open a door or window. Later they will serve no salt or butter as they are on a Pritkin diet.) Republicans think Fettuccini Alfredo is a dead Italian dictator. Democrats think macaroni and cheese is the name of a comedy team.

Republicans think Democrats should keep their noses out of the boardroom. Democrats think Republicans should keep their noses out of the bedroom. Republicans quarrel a lot in private, but put on a unified front in public. Democrats like each other privately, but never let it show in public. Republicans forced to share a bus with reporters don't talk to them. Democrats in the same situation do talk to them. Usually all at once. Republicans are always on time, even for trivial events. Democrats are never on time, even for trivial events. Republicans are receptive to party outsiders as long as they think, dress and act like they do. Democrats welcome outsiders as long as they easily fit into an ethnic, racial or socioeconomic category. If they fit, Democrats nominate them for something. Republican men aren't particular about the suits they wear, as long as they're out of fashion. Democrat men aren't particular about the suits they wear, as long as they've never been in fashion. Republican men keep their coats on at all times because it's "proper." Democrat men keep their coats on only when their shirts are stained.

Democrats prove their commitment to the environment by using paper products made by recycling materials. Republicans prove theirs by staying at hotels without cable television. Republicans usually wear hats and always clean their paint brushes. Democrats give their clothes to the less fortunate. Republicans usually wear theirs. Republicans go out into the countryside to post No Trespassing signs. Democrats bring picnic baskets and start bonfires with the signs. Republicans think brown rice is burnt. Democrats will eat anything with carrots in it—but won't like it much. Republicans hire exterminators. Democrats squash bugs under their heels. Republicans have governesses to care for their children. Democrats have grandmothers. Democrats name their kids after currently popular sports figures, politicians and entertainers. Republicans' offspring are named after their parents or grandparents . . . depending on where the money is.

Albany is filled with Republicans and Democrats—up until 5 P.M. At this point there is a phenomenon much like an automatic dishwasher starting the spin cycle. People begin to pour out of every exit in the city. These are Republicans going home. At the same hour, Democrats flow into every bar for their ginseys at fiveseys. Republicans keep trying to cut down on smoking, but aren't successful. Neither are Democrats. Republicans tend to keep their shades pulled down, although there is seldom a reason why they should. Democrats ought to, but don't. Republicans fish from the sterns of expensive charter boats. Democrats sit on the dock and let the fish come to them. Republicans hide their copies of *Penthouse* inside their *National Star*. Republicans study the financial section of the *New York Times*. Democrats put the section in the bottom of the bird cage. Republican women powder to achieve pallor. Democrat women strive for natural pallor. You're a Republican woman if you wish hats would come back. You're a Democrat woman if you wish hats would go away entirely. On Saturday, Republicans go fox-hunting. Democrats wash the car and get a haircut. There you are. Now make your choice!

——✦——

Walk About Chatham and Be Very Proud

Chatham Village residents should not only stroll through the shops, old and new, that provide them with myriad goods and services, but they should also stretch their legs and take frequent walks about their streets and byways. How long has it been since you climbed up High Street to watch a sunset or gone even higher to explore the village reservoir and enjoy a magnificent view of both the Berkshires and the Catskills?

Walking will not only exhilarate the mind and body, but there is also a pleasure that comes from direct contact with early autumn's flora and fauna. There is joy in reaching a hilltop and viewing the tree-topped Austerlitz hills, the Taconic Parkway snaking north and southward, a ribbon of silver that is the lordly Hudson River, and to the northwest the shimmering white structures that punctuate the City of Albany. There is fun in speculating whose white barn that is over Spencertown way, just what road that green field borders, and are those hickory nut trees in the hedgerow? Have you walked over the Mickle Bridge high above the Steinkill and up Fairview Avenue in that section of the village known for years as "Brooklyn"?

Edge down the slope toward the creek and you will come upon a single grave, the burial site of a young boy who sleeps through eternity in a field of violets. Why he was laid to rest there in this solitary state remains a mystery. Further down the slopes you will find the crumbling vestiges of a Chatham foundry, where, for years on end, you could pick up colorful slugs of what once had been molten materials.

Wander north past the village limits through a rocky and wild ravine where blueberries and evergreens are rich among the rocks. Chatham is not a "pretty village" when compared to picturesque New England villages in the Berkshires. She has had a rough life spawned by millworkers and railroad "gandydancers." For years on end her streets and homes were covered with rail soot belched out by thundering locomotives.

For over a century, our three-story town clock has sounded the hours for families living in magnificent homes occupied by the wealthier Hawley, Seymour, Greene, Payn and White families. It also sounded for the smaller residences that were built along the rail tracks and surrounding the county fairgrounds.

So may we suggest an evening walk down to the Mary E. Dardess and Chatham High school grounds and then along the banks of the Old Pond to hear the bullfrogs in full chorus or observe the water birds gathering their young before emigrating southward as the first frosts of winter approach.

Wildflowers are still in profusion; asters, goldenrod and Queen Anne's lace provide gay bouquets along the water's edge. On occasion, fresh, green clumps of tangy watercress can be found along the pond's banks. Look carefully and you may see the remains of wooden bridges that provided a sylvan walkway through the area, vestigial remains of Stark's Park, which came into being as a WPA project during the depression years. It was later abandoned as the upkeep was too much of a financial burden on the community.

Or, if you are more ambitious, try packing a lunch and, leaving the village, walk in back of the Payn Foundation and climb to the east, then descend down to the Indian Creek and enjoy your repast beside the white waters that plunge along wooded banks toward the Hudson.

You can cross the stream at Arnold's Mills and continue your walk toward Wager Mountain and here you can find a road, still public, but YOUR road, so unused that tufts of grass grow down the very center of this forgotten concourse.

Continue up the mossy slopes of Wager Mountain and stop for a moment to hear the sounds of bees humming in some ancient untended garden patch near the crumbling cellar foundation of a long-forgotten farmhouse. If you know the secret, you can follow the bees to an old tree where rich layers of thick golden honey can be harvested.

Then head homeward crossing back over the summit of Browning's Hill, named for the late Fred Browning who once farmed hundreds of acres overlooking the Punsit Valley. There one can gaze down on Borden's Pond where generations of young Chathamites built bonfires and skated on winter evenings or fished for chub of a summer's day. A splendid civic project is under way to create a wildlife habitat and walking trails around this hidden pearl of water.

Looking down, there are the fairgrounds now silent after last weekend's splendid exhibition came to a close. The fair is gone for another year, but listen closely and you may still hear lilting midway music echoing up from the valley.

No longer can you see the white plume of smoke streaming from the evening train on the Harlem Division nor hear the pounding driverods or the mournful whistle which portended rain by tomorrow. But those of an older generation can still hear and feel the steam engines of our youth. Chatham's lights begin to glow as darkness falls. The fragrance of September sweet grass sweeps up on the evening breeze and a great feeling of serenity and affinity for this little village fills the walker's heart.

No, Chatham may not be a place of beauty, but walk about her these ninth-month days. She's well worth looking at, and she deserves our love, our pride and our affection. After all, she's been very good to all of us over the many years.

＞◆＜

The Day They Buried Old Tom Quinion on Dean Hill

The September winds carried scudding rain clouds over the open pastures on Dean Hill in Canaan on Monday. That was the day they buried 83-year-old Tom Quinion, who, along with his son, William, had grubbed a living on their hillside farm a stone's throw from the Massachusetts border. The men lived alone—without lights, without telephone and without a mail route. That's the way they wanted it. And Thomas Joseph Quinion's funeral was the way he had planned it. Thirty years ago, Mr. Quinion had purchased the former Will Kirby farm in that remote region of Canaan known as Dean Hill. The farmstead is four miles from the nearest road and, at an elevation of 1,550 feet, commanded a magnificent view to the east.

Using only their hands, Tom Quinion and Bill, who is now 53, reclaimed more than 100 acres of farmland that had grown into second-growth woods. When the Kirbys owned Dean Hill they raised hundreds of sheep and the fields were well tended and fertile. Then the wool market collapsed, the sheep were sold off and gradually alders and sumacs sprang from the pastureland. The sun-bathed fields soon were turned into woods.

The only help the Quinions had in this reclamation was a pair of farm horses, "Susan" and "Brownie," and they played a major role in Tom Quinion's funeral. The wind and rain sighed and rustled through acres of hand-planted corn on Monday, when Bill walked out to the barn to hitch up the team to a freshly painted flat-bed farm wagon. He whispered gently as he hitched the traces and then headed for the old home where his father's casket rested.

Tom Quinion desired little in his life. He had few pleasures and he wanted to take a few nice things with him into the next world. As he had wished, his favorite rifle, which had brought down many a deer, was placed beside him along with his battered felt hat, still carrying in the band a partridge feather. There was some candy, some family photos and half a dozen rounds for his rifle. Wherever he was going, Tom was ready.

Some 30 friends and neighbors, the largest gathering of people on Dean Hill in many a year, huddled in the rain beneath a butternut tree, where Bill had dug his father's grave. Bill chirped and carefully backed the team up to the small front door and the casket was placed on the wagon, just the way Tom had wanted. There were two floral pieces under the butternut tree, one evidently from a florist shop. A neat arrangement of mums and gladiolus. Near it was a bright bouquet of zinnias, evidently picked from a neighbor's garden and thrust into a blue glass canning jar. Tom was never much on flowers.

Bill moved the wagon up near the grave and then unhitched Susan and Brownie. His father had wanted the team that had helped him claim his farm to "get a last look at the old man." And the horses did look and Bill gave each one an apple.

Then the Reverend Loren House of the Canaan Congregational Church mounted the wagon which now had a tarpaulin over the ridge poles. Water ran down the pastor's face as he read from the 121st Psalm: "I lift up my eyes to the hills. From whence does my help come? My help comes from the Lord who made heaven and earth."

The Lord had made Dean Hill but it was Tom and Bill and Susan and Brownie who had reclaimed it, and they were together now, in the rain, for the last time. Four husky men, evidently men of the soil, dressed in farm clothes, took the casket and placed it atop the grave.

Supported by planking, the casket rested over the opening while ropes were attached, and then Bill said calmly, "Let 'er down easy." And Tom Quinion was interred in the soil of the farm that he had loved.

No one left for some time. Neighbors, some of whom had smirked at first, now felt the poignancy of the moment. The tenderness that caused the horses to be brought to the casket, the simple grave, the lack of material splendor. The men and women stood and talked about the days when Bill and Tom worked from sunup to sunset, pausing only for a noontime meal in the field or a draught of water from the brook that runs through the farm. They recalled how the older Quinion cooked their meals, in the light of a flickering lantern; they remembered the winters when the Quinions would be isolated for weeks at a time by huge snow drifts that frequently block Dean Hill. On occasion, Bill would come out on snowshoes and hike down five miles to Canaan for provisions and mail. Mail was usually the Sears Roebuck catalogue and the *Chatham Courier*, the only paper they read.

"We're descendants of John Hancock, signer of the Declaration," Tom told a visitor to the farm a few years ago. "I was born in Connecticut and I've been grubbin' the soil all my life. It's tough up here on The Hill. The coons get in the corn, the foxes get in the chickens and dogs chase our cows. But we'll stick it out. It'll take more'n that to drive us out."

And they didn't drive Tom from his land. He died last Thursday in St. Luke's Hospital. The J. A. French Funeral Home of Chatham followed the wishes of the old man and that included that his grave

be "well secured." As his friends drove back over the hill to Rich-
mond, Mass., or down into Canaan, they might have passed a mammoth cement mixing truck. It strained up the rise to the Quinion
farm, moved into place and poured five yards of concrete over Tim
Quinion's coffin. No one is going to move him off Dean Hill for all
eternity. That's the way he wanted it.

SCHOOL DAYS

The Facts of Life Can't Be Hidden

According to a recent survey, half of the state's high school students were reported to be sexually active. As a result, educators are considering sex education classes to begin in the ninth grade and continue through twelfth grade. Children whose parents do not approve may be excused.

I grew up in a simpler time. Only once during my high school career do I recall a girl becoming pregnant, and this was blamed on a hot-blooded stud from Philmont and not on any of us purer-than-the-driven-snow Chatham swain. Chatham kids practiced abstinence simply because they didn't know their way around in what was then a world of primitive sexuality.

Oh, sure, "necking" went on in rumble seats, but to "go all the way" was something you only dreamed about. In the 1930s, sexual education in Chatham High School lasted all of 60 minutes for the entire school year.

It was about this time of year, in early spring, when sap began running in the lads and lassies as well as the maples, that an announcement would be made that a "health assembly" would be held in the school auditorium—one for the boys and a separate one for the girls.

There was an air of dreaded secrecy about these gatherings. At an appointed time, the boys were herded into the auditorium, while Robert F. Aldrich, the school principal, Walter Benson, who taught chemistry and Joel Becker, the school truant officer, stood guard at the doors. Once we were seated, from stage right appeared a small, wizened man, sporting a white goatee and pince-nez glasses. He introduced himself as a doctor and he declared that, in the next 60 minutes, he would teach us all there was to know about S-E-X.

There were snickers and ribald remarks as he described wet dreams, but silence fell over the assembly as the "doctor," now equipped with a foot-long pointer, began to describe wiggly sperm and eggs that were being projected on the screen. No sooner did we learn of our machismo potential than there came a dreaded description of sexually transmitted diseases.

There was syphilis (pronounced *si-fy-lis* by some of the Spencertown boys), with withering photos of what could happen as it advanced through the three phases to systemic infection.

This was followed by an equally dreaded photographic description of gonorrhea, whose bacteria would ravage our bodies. The "doctor" kept referring to this awful malady as "the clap" and laughed uproariously when he reminded us, "Let me tell you one thing, fellows, you don't get it from sitting on a toilet seat." We didn't think it that funny, and by this time we had lost our lust for love-making should the opportunity by some strange circumstance have presented itself.

There followed—and this was the last 10 minutes of the lecture— a treatise on sheaths that males could wear that would impede pregnancies and deter the possibility of being infected by the appalling, debilitating mortifications we had witnessed on the screen. When it was all over, we 15-year-olds were more confused than ever. I recall several of my classmates rushing to the "boys' cloak room" to wash their hands in an effort to rid themselves of possible infections.

The "doctor" gave us fair warning to use "rubbers" should we be smitten with a desire to pursue an amorous maiden. We had seen these things on the rocks at Lampman's Dam, Chatham's favorite swimming hole, but we weren't exactly sure how or when they were used.

As we grew older and in senior high, it was the height of machismo to carry a prophylactic in your wallet. But, when you got home at night, it had to be hidden, lest your parents discover the device. Usually they were stored on the shelf of a locker or hidden in a desk.

Acquiring one was no easy task. Today, condoms in every shape, size, color and design are exhibited as freely as Oh, Henry! or Babe Ruth candy bars were in our younger days. In my youth, they were secreted in some distant part of the store hidden from the public eye. Chatham had three drugstores where they might be purchased. But you just didn't walk in and demand the product in a loud voice. Alvord's Drug Store usually had some female member of the Alvord family on duty and, sure as shootin', you weren't going to ask her.

Harry Branion operated Branion's Drug Store, but he was a straight-laced churchgoer and the last person on earth you would ask to help guard you from the consequences of lustful adventure. McCullough's Drug Store was the answer, because here you could find a colleague in Howard Tubbs, a youth of our own age, who was to become a pharmacist in later life. Howard was a great practical joker and after we had quietly whispered our order, he would shout, "How many rubbers do you want?" startling other customers in the store.

Was all this worth what we hoped would be a moment in amatory paradise?

Back in the halls of Chatham High the girls also had their day in a "health assembly" with some lady who had accompanied the "doctor." The boys were eager to know what was going on in the auditorium, but this time Mary Dardess headed a phalanx of female teachers who kept watch over the auditorium doors lest some eavesdroppers gain knowledge of what was transpiring inside. The girls usually came out blushing and giggling, but there were no revelations except a few, heard second and third hand from guys who had heard it from their "steady" girlfriends. Even then, it was quite confusing.

———≻•⇌———

The Palmer Method

How many of my fellow graduates of Chatham's school system can recall Miss Carmody, who taught the Palmer Method of Writing in the fifth grade? Each mid-morning, Miss Carmody would toss her titian locks and announce firmly, "Now, put your books and papers in your desk and get out your copy books." Desk lids banged and ink well covers flew open.

"Now, remember what I told you yesterday. Hold your pen holder lightly between your thumb and index finger. Don't use it as though you were spearing a potato. Wrist barely touching the desk and use the left side of your hand as a sort of pad which bears the weight. Open to page three. At the top is written 'The big black dog chased Reynard the Fox!' Now, copy this sentence just as you see it written, over and over to the bottom of the page. Ready, tap, tap, tap—round, round, round—write!"

In all country schools across the land this procedure was followed faithfully as an important part of the day's work. Those who learned the Palmer Method were twice blessed. After the eighth grade almost every pupil wrote clearly, and, what was more important, a style of writing that was readable and neat. No right or left slanting of words nor something that looked as if a giant gnat had fallen in the ink bottle, crawled out and dragged itself across the page, spitting as it walked.

Now and then we receive a letter from a young relative who is at college. With the aid of a strong reading glass plus some diligence and imagination, we are, after a day or so, able to decipher his hieroglyphics. Still another relative, in her 30s, was never taught or cared to learn how to join letters together. She's still in the printing stage.

The faithful shining steel nib, which was wiped clean after use with a homemade pen wiper, will soon be a collector's item. Pen wipers were made by doting aunts or grandmothers and were an important part of a pencil box. The pencil box, pride of every beginner, is also just a memory. I still have an old-fashioned pen in which the steel nibs can be inserted. I can remember going into E. B. Reynolds' store on Main Street (before Delson's) and ordering a pack of "Probate" nibs.

While at Crossgates Mall recently, I stopped in a stationery store and inquired of a callous young clerk about these pen points. He said he had never heard of such things. After carefully enlightening him as to what they were, he scornfully announced, "Well, I guess that dates you!" Perhaps it does, but I'll wager a ream of foolscap and two goose quills that I can write a clearer and more legible "hand" than he does.

Teachers! Let's go back to the days of Palmer Method, at least as far as writing in concerned, and while you're at it, you might look into a new method of teaching spelling.

━━➤◆⇐━━

Little Red Schoolhouse

On one of those sun-filled, blue-sky days we had before Hurricane Bertha deluged us with rain, we drove over to see the Rider's Mills schoolhouse, a gem of early-American architecture in its peaceful setting above the Kinderhook Creek on Rider's Mills Road. We are pleased to observe that, in spite of sustaining two centuries of winter's cold and summer's heat, the handsome little structure seems to be holding its own.

Horace Peaslee, the noted architect who designed several major buildings in Washington, D.C., the Eisenhower gardens in Gettysburgh, Pa., and Chatham's Tracy Memorial Village Hall, thought it one of the finest examples of an early rural school in the nation. Peaslee, once a resident of Malden Bridge, was instrumental in having the school's plans included in the Library of Congress' archives. It is said the school was the first to be built with state funding, in 1795.

Interesting features of architectural note are the school's barrel-shaped ceiling and thick walls of English brick. There is only one other known barrel-shaped ceiling in an early school and that is in Williamsburg, Va.

Years ago, I received a letter from Mrs. Carrie Coffin Presson who attended classes at the school in the late 1870s. She wrote: "The desks were long, painted board tables with nearby benches for seats. You speak of lights, I think all we had was what the Lord gave us—daylight and sunlight. The school room was heated with a large wood stove and our water supply was a large tin bucket with a long-handled dipper."

Mrs. Fowler Root, who can count 101 winters, once served as a substitute teacher. Her husband, the late Fowler Root, was schoolmaster for 39 years. Mrs. Root recalls the school as a part of Chatham's School District 3, one of many districts throughout the township before consolidation.

"Most of the pupils were local children and most of them walked long distances each day to class. The school day began at 9 A.M., followed by a 15-minute morning recess and an hour's break at noon.

The lunches, usually sandwiches, were brought in brown paper bags. Then classes resumed and continued until 4 P.M. In the winter months, the children walked home in the gathering darkness. We had [a] rather complete curriculum from the first to the eighth grade," Mrs. Root recalls.

Youngsters who continued on to high school had a long day before them. They would arise at dawn and go to Old Chatham, where they would board the Rutland Railroad train to Chatham. The Rutland station was at the corner of Park Row and Kinderhook Street in the village, and each morning students from New Lebanon, Brainard, Rayville, Old Chatham and Rider's Mills would walk down Kinderhook Street to the Woodbridge Avenue school and then reverse the procedure every evening.

A number of years ago, the Rider's Mills Historical Association was formed. Its purpose is the preservation of the school located at the intersection of Rider's Mills Road and Pitt Road. The association is chartered by the Board of Regents of the State of New York. The present officers are John B. Carroll of Malden Bridge, president; Richard Dorsey, Esq., of Malden Bridge, vice president; John Doyle, Jr., of Malden Bridge, secretary; and Robert G. Leary of Old Chatham's RD, treasurer. In addition to its regular meeting, the association offers a number of programs at the school, all of which are open and free to the public.

Those who visit the school will find its interior little changed since the day it closed in 1954. Students' desks are in evidence along with that of the schoolmaster, while blackboards and chalk erasers can be seen. Outside, the omnipresent outhouse—one side for girls, the other for boys—still stands nearby now cloaked with woodbine.

As we drove away over the narrow, country road, and out to Route 66, perhaps we heard the laughter and shouts of boys and girls in the school yard during recess. Then a bell rang, the chatter stopped and the pupils returned to the 3 R's under the tutelage of Lucas Schermerhorn, Ida Thorne, Mr. and Mrs. Fowler Root or many other pedagogues who taught generations of rural youngsters.

⇒·◇·⇐

The Great Christmas Tree Caper—60 Years Ago

We are in the midst of the season to be merry, floated on a hot buttered rum: "A spoonful of brown sugar, one clove, a jigger of ripe Jamaican rum (make that a jigger and a half, ho, ho, ho), a lump of butter as big as a hazelnut. Fill a six-ounce glass with steaming hot water. And, as the butter melts, top with a dash of nutmeg." God bless us, one and all.

In the frosty night, the stars are pinpoints of ice. Above the street, the littlest angel flies on wired wings. The carillon in the church tower chimes *Silent Night*. Each note is full and frosted. Globes of Christmas music to cheer the weary and encourage the wicked.

"Batteries not included." We shopped up to the last blessed moment. The battery-powered doll comes when you call her. "Battery included" takes some of the magic off the Christmas toy. Replacement batteries are a gimmick. My boys never turned off anything they turned on. They just let the batteries run downnnnnnnnnnnn-n-n- . . . After a while, I ran down to Delson's, almost daily.

When I was a child, window shopping the wonderful world of toys, batteries were something my grandfather put in the flashlight. We ran our toys with elbow grease. The toy cannon did not fire anything. Batteries were not included, for there was no place to put them. There was no remote switch to control them, only by our imagination. We pushed the cannon into position and hollered "BANG!" We saluted each other: "I will volunteer, sir."

A battery-operated artillery-man would probably say: "Who, me?"

The carillon music rises to the iced stars. *Holy Night.*

You've-heard-it-before-dept: requests have once again poured in to tell the tale of the purloined Christmas tree, so here it is on the 60th anniversary.

In my youth there were no $30 Christmas trees that came to Chatham from such faraway places as Split Lip, Oregon. You went out in the woods and cut your own. December 16, 1931, lives on as a day of infamy in the old Chatham Union School District, for that was the fatal day when four striplings volunteered to provide a Christmas tree for Mrs. Inez Francisco's sixth grade. "The girls will decorate the tree, if I can have some boys volunteer to get it," said Mrs. Francisco. Harold Ludington's arm shot up first, followed by Robert Sayer's, James Harding's and yours truly. For this service, I envisioned at last a C in arithmetic on my next report card. I had failed that hateful subject in the last marking period.

Time was of the essence. The tree had to be in the schoolroom the next day, and such lovely nubile maidens as Helen Golden, Helen Brenon, Marion Cole and Laura Navarra were already busy making foil angels to hang on its branches. It was agreed among the volunteers that we would dash home to get rope, hatchets, saws, fetch sled and other accouterments necessary to fell the tree. The December sun was fading in the western sky when we met at the corner of Hudson Ave. and Coleman Street to begin our adventure. Harold Ludington had suggested "Snake Hole" on the Indian Creek as an excellent site, for the area was filled with pine trees. To reach Snake Hole meant climbing Browning's Hill toward Spencertown, then descending down the opposite side to the creek.

By now it was 4:30 and almost dark. We started out, but as we passed the Payn Foundation, I recalled there was a "Christmas tree" on the hillside opposite the home. Why walk all the way to Snake Hole when we have this fine blue spruce within hatchet's reach?

Within minutes we topped the tree and congratulated ourselves on the time-saving, picture-perfect selection. Bob Sayer, who lived on Library Place, agreed to take the tree to his house just a stone's throw from the Woodbridge Ave. school. Mrs. Francisco was jubilant when she saw the splendidly symmetrical spruce elevated into position by the proud foursome who had caused its downfall.

Sixty years ago there was a competition among the grades for the best class Christmas tree. Professor A. Wesley Armitage, the school principal, would judge the entries. We knew we had a winner. The girls had done a magnificent job in decorating the evergreen and, in due time, Professor Armitage arrived. "This is a beautiful tree," he declared in announcing the sixth grade as the winner. Cheers almost drowned out his next fateful question, "Where did it come from?" The four volunteers shot knowing glances at each other and James Harding, who later became an attorney, showed youthful legal and prudent potentials when he replied, "Oh, over toward Browning's Hill."

While the sixth grade celebrated its triumph, other fearsome forces were at work. The caretaker at the Payn Home noted that a blue spruce had been topped and some meddlesome person reported having seen four small boys hauling a tree down Coleman St. in yesterday's gathering gloom. Law and order worked with lightning speed in those days. Before the sixth graders had finished their celebratory hot cocoa, Christmas cookies and anise drops, Sgt. Gary Sager of the New York State Police was in Professor Armitage's office. The troopers in 1931 rode horseback through the countryside and stabled their mounts in a barn on Hudson Ave., convenient to a great Victorian home where they resided.

Sgt. Sager toured the classrooms and only one had a magnificent blue spruce. It didn't take him long to put one and one together. Great joy in providing the best tree in the school suddenly turned to fear and trepidation. That night, I confessed to my father about my part, and Father's decision was immediate: "Call Sgt. Sager on the phone and tell him what you've done."

Parental orders were obeyed without question in those days and I admitted my trespasses to Sgt. Sager, who replied, " I want to see you in Judge Pratt's office tomorrow, right after school." Thank goodness he hadn't asked me to identify my compatriots. When I told my pals, "I'm going alone," they wouldn't dream of my taking the rap solo, we'd been buddies for too long—through too many adventures together—it simply wouldn't do. "We're going with you," they pronounced, almost drowning out the audible sound of banging knees.

Judge Pratt was a small man who looked 100 years old in my mind. He was a stonecutter who carved doves, angels and names of the departed on the gravestones that stood in rows where Watts' Jewelry is now located. The judge and his whole office were perennially covered in a thin layer of white dust, giving him the appearance of already having gone to the Great Beyond.

We expected the worst, but Judge Pratt began to regale us with stories of his misspent youth—tipping over outside toilets; hauling a farm wagon to the roof ridge of Woodman's Hall; applying tar to the town clock bell rope, which caused firemen to be hauled heavenward when they sounded the village alarm. He finally gave us a severe warning, but smiled through his gray mask and admitted in his high voice, "I was a boy once myself."

So ended one of the most nefarious deeds ever committed at Chatham Union School; but the story doesn't end there. The next time you're at the First National parking lot, look to the hillside

47

opposite the Payn Home. There, silhouetted against the sky, is a great blue spruce with a most irregular, rough, snaggy top. You can almost imagine that someone lopped it off when the tree was very, very young.

HISTORY NOTES

Remember Those Good OLD Days?

Brushing aside the cobwebs of years gone by, your old scrivener will seek to recall memories of bygone events, names, places and day-to-day happenings of what we gray-haired old folks like to call "the good old days." For example, do you remember when the highlights of every senior year at Chatham High were the annual trip to Washington, D.C., and the senior play? . . . When every well-dressed man in Chatham had his suits made by Chris Christensen, whose tailor shop was on Main St. . . . When Beezie B. Connor, Chatham Union School's second-grade teacher, arrived every morning on the train from Philmont, and headed off to class with a jar of honey for her persistent cough . . . When you could dine and dance at The Edgewood in East Greenbush and come home with change from a $10 bill . . . Frankie Carle's orchestra helped make it a memorable evening . . . Or you could also do the shag or twist around in a conga line at Dance-O-Land in Brainard or The Showboat in New Lebanon . . . When in the summer of 1957, a scrawny kid with a long nose, made her first-ever theatre appearance in "Teahouse of the August Moon" at the Malden Bridge Playhouse? Her name: Barbra Streisand. When Chatham village enjoyed weekly concerts played by the Chatham Post 42, American Legion Band or musicians under the baton of the Reverend Charles Witthoft, entertained on Park Row?

When on an April's eve you could enjoy a delicious boned shad whose skeletal framework had been removed by Harold Archer of

Archer's Market on Main St. . . . He offered to pay $1 for every bone you found . . . When Peter Gross ran a small grocery store at the corner of Church St. and Hudson Ave., and, on the opposite corner, George Stark pumped gasoline and sold the world's most powerful horseradish? . . . When the best cheese in the county was purveyed by Bernie Redmond at the Old Chatham Country Store? . . . When the favorite haunt for service personnel on leave during WW II was the Van Hoesen House in Niverville? . . . When Albany families came by train on Sundays to dine at the Stanwix Hotel or the Chatham House? . . . Six-course dinners cost $1.50.

When, on hot summer days you cycled up Browning's Hill and then walked through daisy-strewn fields to swim at "Snake Hole" on the Indian Creek . . . (The place was aptly named as there were as many black snakes as swimmers in the deep, dark waters.) . . . When the Borden Milk Company operated milk collecting stations at Old Chatham and Buckleyville. Ice was cut from Borden's Pond in Chatham and hauled by horse-drawn sleds to Buckleyville for loading aboard rail cars which carried the milk to New York City . . . When the Foley Dog Shows were held at the Chatham Fairgrounds, bringing the best of the canine world to our village?

When every Chatham High maiden wore a white middy blouse, a flowing black tie and black bloomers during gym classes that were held by Elvira Dean Pulver ? . . . When the greatest event at the BIG Chatham Fair was the annual 2.22 County Trot which pitted Tom Buckley of Buckleyville in the sulky behind Bold Ruler against Doug Mansfield of Philmont and his fine trotter, Bright Star? . . . When presidential candidates would pass through Chatham and step out on the platform of their observation cars to wave at Chathamites? Al Smith, Harry Truman and Dwight D. Eisenhower thus greeted their followers . . . When the great social event of the year was the American Legion Past Commander's Ball at the Morris Memorial?

In 1930, dancers glided about the gym floor to the music of Paul Whiteman's orchestra and in 1933 Vincent Lopez and his orchestra did the honors . . . When, if the weather was bad and you couldn't walk home for lunch, you carried a brown bag of comestibles to the Woodbridge Ave. school that reeked of damp clothing, peanut butter, as well as skunk or horse manure on farm boys' boots? . . . Do you remember when the last Harlem Division train at night, returning from New York City, would crawl up Hudson Ave., so conductors, brakemen and other crew members could hop off and go directly home?

When Chatham's one-man police force in the person of Chief Frank Ward would lock up miscreants in a jail in the Tracy Memorial cellar? . . . When Dr. Frank Maxon Sr. was a most imposing figure riding his horse from his stable on Kinderhook Street out into the countryside? . . . When Morton Tank grew fabulous flowers in his greenhouses over in "Brooklyn" as Chathamites called the west side of the Stein Kill creek? . . . When the corner of Park Row and Kinderhook St. was flooded with students headed for Chatham Union School, arriving on the Rutland Railroad local from New Lebanon, Brainard and Old Chatham? . . . When the sound of a smithy's hammer rang out on River Street as Harry Cole shod the best of Chatham's horseflesh . . . When in the summer of 1943, during WW II, Charlie Wyman, one of Chatham's young Army Air Corps pilots, "buzzed" the village, which caused "Colonel" Henry Alvord, the community's chief air-raid warden, to activate the village's alarm in the event of an enemy attack—the steam whistle on the old railroad roundhouse. When the best free lunch during the depression was served by Herm Engelke in the basement bar at the Hoffman House? . . . When more than 150 women were employed at the Chatham Shirt Factory on Church Street? . . . When one-legged "Hopper" Wilber marched and played in the Ghent Band

and, at Chatham fair time, took on the best wrestlers who came along with the fair's sideshows? . . . And do you recall when cigar-smoking Madame Soller played in the Ghent Band? . . . When the Sultan of Swat, Babe Ruth, would come up every fall from Gotham to go bird shooting with Colin Macfarlane in Canaan, and then enjoy collations and libations at Pete Berry's hotel? . . . When a giant of a man who announced trains at the Albany Union Station would intone . . . "All out for the Pittsfield local on Track 5 with stops at Rensselaer, Brookview, Niverville, THEY NEVER WORKED AND THEY NEVER WILL, Chatham Center, Chatham, etc."

Remember when the *Chatham Courier*'s phone number was 15 and subscriptions were $2.50 a year? . . . Times have changed!

Daylight-Saving Time Ends

We're back on God's time, and just in time. November approached signaling pre-Christmas sales. We are going to have an election and trust a lot of people will come. Wise people keep saying, "You can't turn the clock back," but that's what we did as daylight-saving time ended. Somewhere, in the middle of the night, we got back the hour we lost last April, or did we? I don't feel that we got an extra hour of sleep, do you? When an hour's gone, it's gone, and that's that. Anybody who tells you differently is just another lying politician. I prefer the beginning of DST because it happens in the spring, base-ball is just around the corner, the saps are running, the juice is rising and you only have to advance your clocks and watches one hour.

When it ends, you turn the clocks back, and if they're electronic, it's not all that easy. You have to go all around the dial, and turning a watch back is supposed to be bad for the works. I've got around 20 clocks and watches, so I spent a busy Sunday. So did a lot of other people, all of them dialing the operator for the correct time or picking it up on Channel 7, Chatham's own time, weather and current events station.

Now that we've demonstrated it's possible to turn back the clock, why don't we keep turning it back to the good old times? As in a bad movie, the scene gradually changes as the hands whirl around in reverse. Magically, we are young again. There are parking spaces everywhere, even on Main Street at high noon on Saturdays. There are rich people and poor but not so many of them. Now and then it even rains, but always just before dawn and the daylight hours are heavenly. You can throw a silver dollar on Herm Engelke's bar at the Hoffman House, order a bourbon old fashioned and get six bits in change. *Six bits:* that's a term as dead as the silver dollar, which, by the way, was almighty and respected the world around, the same globe that was covered by Sherwin-Williams Paints.

As long as we're about it, let's turn the clock back to tea dancing. As a social and presexual exercise, the tea dance was an excellent way of getting together. A drink and a dance at the end of the day— is that so bad? During the '20s through the '40s, tea dancing was big from the great hotel rooms to racier gin mills. The guys wore their hair pomaded and their suits nipped at the waist and were known as "snakes." The flappers showed lots of garter and loved to Charleston. I remember tea dancing at the Ledge in Albany's DeWitt Clinton Hotel where the Three Suns played and at the Edgewood where band leader Frankie Carl tinkled the ivories. One of the best things about tea dancing was that hardly anybody drank tea. We could live without the creamed chicken in patty shells, too.

Yes, my eyes are glazing over. Daylight Saving has ended, the spell is broken, there isn't a parking space to be found and there's that damned election coming up. The weather continues to be relentlessly perfect. Blue skies and not a cloud in sight at this writing. The mercury hit 77 today, a record for late October.

The trees are divesting themselves of their leaves, brown now instead of brilliant reds and golds. Stark, empty tree limbs jut skyward like gnarled fingers. Soon November will rule a land turned ice cold as we turn the 11th page of the calendar. But for now, the light keeps changing as you move along in and out of the sunshine. From minute to minute, a complete microseason. No wonder the tourists are fascinated by Columbia County. No wonder we old timers never fall out of love with her, even when she breaks your heart and sometimes your head. And so we head into deep fall, which doesn't mean necessarily that winter is around the corner. Forget about the time and the season and live it the way it was meant to be lived—day by day. See you at the tea dance.

Just for the fun of it, let's try turning the clocks back, not just an hour, but let's pick a number—42 years—and here we are in the summer of 1949. In June of that year, Dean Goodman, a young producer, brought a number of Hollywood stars to the Crandell, which was transformed into a straw-hat circuit theater. Chathamites oohed and ahhed at Glenda Farrell, Ann Harding, and Helmut Dantine. These luminaries didn't draw well and so the theater turned to musicals. The first production was "On the Town" and it brought together a number of kids who were all but stranded in Chatham. Perhaps older readers may remember an exciting blonde, Jo Hurt or sultry Ruth Webb, whose name was later to be linked with a number of B'way stars. There was Jonathan Lucas, who would go on to become one of the nation's leading choreographers. Three "local youngsters" were identified in a playbill as Muriel Scott, now Muriel Faxon of MacHaydn Theater fame, George Vosburgh, Jr., who danced his way from the Lucky Strike Hit Parade to Hollywood, where he is currently producing the top TV game show, *Jeopardy,* and Lena Devich, well, what ever happened to Lena??? . . . The young players also staged *Best Foot Forward, Laff That Off* and the season closed with Ernest Truex enacting his original Broadway role in *George Washington Slept Here*. . . . After a farewell party at the then popular East Room in the Chatham House, the thespians left town, some to fame, some to oblivion.

And 1949 was a good year for summer stages at other theaters. Buster Keaton, Kay Francis, Mady Christians and Lewis Roerick were at the Berkshire Playhouse in Stockbridge. At Malden Bridge Playhouse, Peggy and Walter Wood opened with *The Bat,* starring Mary Elizabeth Aurelius, who later went on to several good roles on Broadway. Top seats that year, by the by, were $1.25 and $2.10 . . . After theater, you could dance at the Showboat in New Lebanon to Tony Pastor's band or square dance with Jerry and Sky at Dance-O-Land. Cuba libres, a mixture of Coca Cola and rum, were the most popular drink that summer. A tall, cool one cost 45 cents. Dr. Serge Koussevitsky arrived at Lenox with the Boston Symphony Orchestra to open their eighth summer season at Tanglewood. The most popular movies were John Wayne in *Stagecoach* and Bing Crosby in *Pennies From Heaven*. . . . Gil's Diner in New Lebanon offered this "weekend special": a pitcher of beer and a roast beef dinner for $1.50 . . . Saratoga Harness track presented "The Chatham" as one of its Grand Circuit feature races with a purse of $5,000. It's now over $50,000. And before the snow fell, Cornelia Otis Skinner would open the Chatham Community Entertainment Series, a program sponsored by local organizations. All in all, it was a very good year, if you care to admit your age. Now let's reset those clocks to the present.

A Reunion of General Patton's 'Lucky Few'

In a few days, I will depart for New Orleans to attend a reunion of officers who served in Headquarters, Third Army, in 1944–45 under the command of General George S. Patton, Jr. My army service with Third Army began in March 1944 when I arrived at his headquarters in the English midlands in the picturesque village of Knutsford. I had been detached from the 66th Infantry Division at Camp Robinson, Arkansas and my duties with the U.S. Army Counter-Intelligence Corps, and given orders to serve overseas with another unnamed CIC detachment. My trans-Atlantic crossing on the old Cunard liner, *Mauritania,* was spent in sardine can–like existence with 5,500 other service personnel. Arriving in Knutsford, I was directed to the G-2 intelligence office to present my orders. The room was empty except for one desk behind which sat a squinty-eyed, hawk-beaked, half-pint lieutenant colonel with a squeaky, raspy voice.

"Lieutenant," he snapped, "you are at the Headquarters, Third United States Army, commanded by General George S. Patton, Jr., and if you so much as mention that fact to anyone, your ass is grass."

Thus was my first meeting with Lt. Col. Horace Franklin, who would be my commanding officer for the next two years, and later, by coincidence, my good neighbor and friend in Old Chatham, where he lived out his retirement years.

The warning, not to mention the general's name, was part of the role Patton would play in decoying the Germans. Although the invasion was scheduled to take place on the beaches of Normandy, elaborate steps were being taken to give German intelligence sources the impression that Patton's army would land in the Pas de Calais area, much further east. The Germans fell for the hoax and built up a major force there to halt "Armegruppe Patton." Colonel Franklin told me to be ready at 0800 the next morning to attend General Patton's daily briefing. The briefing was held in a large hall with more than 100 officers present. We rose when the commanding general entered from a side door and remained at rigid attention until we were put at ease. I stared in awe at this man whose face was set in an almost ferocious scowl. The chin thrust forward aggressively, the corners of the mouth turned down, and a hard glint shone from narrowed eyes. Patton called this hard-as-nails look his "war face." It was not a look that came to him naturally. By his own admission, he had practiced it in front of a mirror throughout his life.

Consider, for example, his uniform. From head to toes, everything was spit and polish. His helmet gleamed brilliantly, the result of dozens of coats of varnish. His jacket fit him perfectly. The stars designating his rank, as well as the brass buttons, sparkled; rows of campaign ribbons lent a bright splash of color. Around his waist was a broad leather belt and at his hips, a pair of ivory-handled pistols that were his trademark. Standing tall and erect, chest out, shoulders back, he was an imposing figure.

Patton's showmanship was not just a matter of appearance. He was a master of profanity and prided himself on being able to "cuss out" a man for two or three minutes without having to repeat a single swear word. His "pep talks" to his troops were laced with the rawest of language. A mild example is this statement made to his men shortly before the invasion of Sicily.

"Now, I want you to remember that no son-of-a-bitch ever won a war by dying for his country. He won it making the other poor son-of-a-bitch die for his country." All these things—the angry scowl, the arrogant bearing, the pistol at his hips, the brutal exhortations to spill blood, the cursing and butt-kicking—had a definite purpose. They were intended to create the impression that General George S. Patton was the toughest, meanest soldier in this man's army.

It certainly didn't fool Patton's boss, General Dwight D. Eisenhower, Supreme Commander of the Allied Forces in Europe. In his book, *Crusade in Europe,* Eisenhower assesses Patton in these words:

> All of his mannerisms he developed were of his own adoption. One of his poses, for example, was that he was the most hard-boiled individual in the Army. Actually, he was soft-hearted . . . that was possibly his greatest fault.

One can cite many instances of Patton's soft-heartedness. On one occasion, for example, Patton was riding in an open command car near Colmar, France, in freezing weather. Noticing his driver was shivering, Patton asked the man if he was wearing a warm sweater. When the driver replied, "No, Sir," Patton peeled off his own sweater and gave it to him.

One of my favorite personal recollections of the general was shortly after Third Army was activated on August 1, 1944, and was forging south through Normandy toward the village of Avranches. Wrecked and burning German vehicles left by retreating German forces blocked every road. Patton would tolerate no delay. At Avranches, an armored division had stalled before a river and a small group of us watched as the commanding general studied a map to find a spot where the river might be shallow enough to cross. At that moment, Patton pulled up in a jeep, hopped out, heard of the delay and then waded into the stream himself, looked at some Germans a short distance away, and then returned. "OK," he said to the general, "take them across. This sewer isn't more than two feet deep."

During Third Army's historic American "blitz" across Europe, its corps and divisions liberated or conquered more than 82,000 square miles of territory including 1,500 cities and towns, captured in battle 956,000 enemy soldiers and killed or wounded at least 50,000 others. France, Belgium, Luxembourg, Germany, Austria and Czechoslovakia bear witness to these exploits. On December 9, 1945, while riding with his chief of staff on the way to a pheasant hunt, an army truck coming in the opposite direction collided with Patton's car. The impact fractured the general's neck and he died 12 days later. His remains are buried in an American military cemetery in Luxembourg, joining 6,000 other Third Army heroes. In death, Patton would be eternally near the battlefield, among the soldiers of his command. Where once there were hundreds of officers on Patton's staff, our ranks have been greatly reduced to 89, and only 22 will attend the reunion. His code name for Headquarters, Third Army, in the field was "Lucky" and the old soldiers who will gather for the last time have dubbed themselves "The Lucky Few." On November 11 we will mark the 117th date of Patton's birth and we'll lift a glass to our old commanding officer, who must be ranked in the forefront of America's greatest military leaders.

⋙◆⋘

The Days When the Klan Held Sway in Chatham

At this writing, as election day approaches, the media is caterwauling that we can expect "dirty campaigning" throughout New York State and the nation. Dirty, my foot. These adolescent news anchors should have been around in the autumn of 1928 when the Republicans nominated Herbert Clark Hoover, a Quaker, as their candidate for president and the Democrats selected Governor Alfred E. Smith of New York. Smith was the first communicant of the Roman Catholic Church to seek the presidency and, as a result, a bitter, turbulent, frenzied period of American political life ensued. The anti-Catholic forces contended that if Governor Smith was elected, "The Pope would run the United States government." There were many militant splinter groups opposing Governor Smith that autumn of 1928, but none as vehement as the Ku Klux Klan.

Chatham was a hotbed for the Klansmen, and many prominent village residents secretly donned the white-hooded robes in the driving desire to keep Smith out of the White House.

The Klan's headquarters 74 years ago was in the present building occupied by the MacHaydn Theater. The structure, during the World War I period, was the site of the Caxton Printing Company, but the firm closed its doors in 1927. At the height of the Hoover-Smith campaign, the building became the Kline Kill Klub, a not too subtle way of concealing the fact that it was now the base of operation for the KKK.

As election day neared, posters attacking not only Governor Smith, but all who professed the Roman Catholic faith, appeared on trees and utility poles in Chatham and its environs. Vicious hate mail condemning Catholics filled mail boxes. Although it could not be proven, many believed that local government and police officials of the day were pro-KKK, and thus venomous diatribes continued unabated.

I recall going with my family, as a boy of 10, one evening in September to visit my grandfather at his Valatie residence. My mother was driving, and as we left Chatham on what is now Route 203, there were torches placed in the road. In the glare of these fiery signals we could see a line of hooded men in the traditional Klan garb forming a chain across what was then a dirt road. They halted our car as we approached and signaled my mother to roll down the window. As she did, they thrust a handful of papers into the car including more anti-Catholic propaganda—and, brazenly, a list of Klan meetings, and when and where they would be held. A few nights later, on Labor Day evening we attended the closing night of the Chatham Fair. There was a brilliant display of fireworks for the fair's finale and while bombs burst in air, the Ghent Band played the National Anthem.

At the very last bar there was a loud detonation on Browning's Hill opposite the grandstand and immediately the outline of a burning cross seared the darkness. Some people cheered, but the majority sat horrified at the spectacle.

Late October, my father, who was one of the county's great orators, was asked to give a historical address at the Red Rock Methodist Church. Although a steadfast Republican, he avoided the sensitive issues of the campaign and recalled the annals of the New England Yankees who settled in Red Rock, hailing their diligence and patriotism. After a light collation was served, the audience prepared to leave the church. As my father descended the church steps, there again was an explosion on an opposite hill, and once more, a huge fiery cross lit the night sky.

"Apparently they didn't like what I said," my father observed. With that, a man who neither my father nor any member of the audience had ever seen, stepped out of the darkness and said, "On the contrary, we did!" He immediately disappeared into the night.

Mr. Hoover won the election that year and the Klan lost its momentum. During the campaign, Al Smith made a brief stop in Chatham and addressed a crowd of his followers from the rear of a special railroad observation car. The event came off without incident. Today, the Klan is so tiny that if you really knew how few, you wouldn't take them any more seriously than you do people who cover their bodies with tattoos.

It's only when the media takes the bait you'll see headlines like "Racist Rally—Officials Say Klan Not Wanted Here." The Klan will get 10 new members from that headline. If people get out to demonstrate against them, they'll get 20 new members. If someone commits an act of violence against the Klan, that's 40 members. If someone commits an act of violence against a policeman who's defending the Klan's right to assemble, that's 50 members. If the *New York Times* shows up, that's 200 members. If you ignore the Klan, it withers and dies. The hooded hooligans know how the game is played. When are the media people going to wise up?

⇒·◦·⇐

He Shook the Hand of Abraham Lincoln

A visit to the Louis F. Payn Foundation in Chatham this week brought back a flood of childhood memories. I was raised in the shadow of the original Payn residence, a rambling Victorian structure with wrap-around porches and two-story turrets reaching skyward.

My family home, the present Wenk Funeral Home, at 21 Payn Avenue, bordered the extensive Payn property. A map at the Payn Foundation shows that Mr. Payn owned hundreds of acres stretching eastward from Payn Avenue to the Indian Creek, two miles distant.

Louis Frisbee Payn was born in the Town of Ghent in 1835. The place of his birth, a farm on Route 66, was designated a historic site and a marker stood for many years beside the highway. It was knocked down one winter by a snowplow and never replaced. At the age of eight, he moved with his family to Chatham and the village would be his principal place of residence until his death in 1923 at the age of 88. Mr. Payn was a wealthy man when he died, but did not accrue his financial fortune until late in life. It was not until he was in his 60s that he invested in a plan to purchase a huge tract of land in Oklahoma where oil might be found. Sure enough, oil gushed from the earth and he was suddenly rich.

Mr. Payn did not covet his newly found fortune but rather was deeply concerned with the welfare of all about him. He was personally involved in community affairs, especially when he felt there was a need for his help. He equipped the auditorium in the then-new Chatham Union School on Woodbridge Avenue with seats, stage curtains and drapes. He made possible the building of the Payn AME Church on High Street and Chatham Central Scholarships, named for his widow. Payn's Mills, about two miles east of Chatham, now the Columbia Corporation, provided employment for many in the manufacture of paperboard products. The settlement there is still known as Payn's Mills.

There are many heartwarming tales of his varied philanthropies. One is that, in a time of great need, when Chathamites literally did not have enough to eat, he had a carload of potatoes and other staples shipped in and distributed to the hungry. He also encouraged people to help themselves. He divided a portion of his land into small garden plots, for children to plant, tend and raise their own vegetables. How proud were the winners of the coveted prizes for the best gardens which he personally awarded each year at the Chatham Fair.

In his later years, Mr. Payn enjoyed riding in his open touring car, driven by Harry Waltermire of Ghent. When he came to a group of children, he would toss out a handful of coins. The kids loved it, but the village fathers judiciously asked him to refrain, lest some child be injured as they rushed into the street for the coppers. Mrs. Payn delighted in directing village children in little plays staged at the Payn residence. Christmastime was his great delight, and he was known to have said that no needy family in Chatham would be without a basket of Yuletide goodies.

The large and imposing home at the corner of Payn Avenue and Coleman Street was one of several residences owned by the Payns. Their winter retreat was "Paynhurst," then considered the showplace of Bermuda. To it each year went the Payns, with a retinue of servants and their families. Harry Waltermire had the task of loading five horses, "three sets of Coveys harness" from Mr. Covey's harness shop in Chatham and a four-in-hand coach aboard a New York-bound train and then onto a steamer to Bermuda. The family would then escape Columbia County winters to enjoy the beautiful drives that Bermuda had to offer.

The Payns also maintained a summer home in Malden Bridge where he raised horses on what was later the Hoellerich Farm on Route 66. When the farm was sold to Tom Martin of Old Chatham, it reverted to its original purpose. Louis Payn would have liked that.

Mr. Payn was responsible for the establishment of a strong Republican Party in Columbia County. He was not only the local leader, but was a strategist and kingmaker on the state and national levels. He served in various public capacities. He was named State Superintendent of Insurance by Governor Frank Black and United States Marshall by President U. S. Grant.

There was a twice-told story that after the presidential election of 1888 when Samuel J. Tilden of New Lebanon, a Democrat, won the popular vote, only to lose to Republican Rutherford B. Hayes in the Electoral College, it was feared that Tilden forces might try to create a public uprising and seize the presidency.

It is said a courier from President Grant arrived in Chatham and delivered a sealed envelope to Marshall Payn. In it was an executive order to arrest Tilden on sight should he attempt to interfere with the election results. The papers were never served.

He was a delegate to state and national Republican conventions when his political perspicuity led to the nomination of not only governors but presidents. He was, however, "his own man" and for a time was at odds with Theodore Roosevelt, after Roosevelt bolted the Republican Party to run as a Bull Moose Party candidate in 1912. Roosevelt later sought to bury the hatchet and asked if he could come to Chatham to see Payn. A date was set by Mr. Payn and it was in early September during the Chatham Fair. Payn arranged for Roosevelt to speak and it was agreed the former president would admit his error in bolting the Republican Party and as he did, Mr. Payn sat on the platform, a slight smile of triumph crossing his face.

Mr. Payn's interest in the welfare of his fellow man is perhaps best exemplified in the provision for the Payn Foundation. It had long been his dream to provide a home for local residents and the plans were being developed when he died. The work, however, went forward under the direction of his widow and a board chosen by her. The huge Victorian house was razed and on 12 acres of land on Coleman Street in Chatham was erected the attractive brick dwelling which served as home for some 25 Columbia County residents.

In the foyer of the main residence is a portrait of Mr. Payn by Samantha Huntley, a Kinderhook portrait painter, and it is Mr. Payn as I remember him. Small of stature but solidly built, he had bright pink cheeks, white hair and a small white goatee.

I was probably five years of age when I made a daily trek to the Payn residence. Mr. Payn was bedridden at the time, but I was admitted by a Swiss maid each day and allowed into the Marshall's bedroom. I remember him propped up with pillows, wearing a nightshirt, his pink cheeks glowing as he greeted me in a slightly raspy voice. He was always glad to see me as we shared a little secret. Each morning he would be served porridge, which he detested. He would hand me the plate and I would quickly consume the contents and put it back on his bed. For this, I would receive a few pennies for my gourmandizing. The maid would arrive a few minutes later and say, "Ah. Mr. Payn, fine, you've eaten everything." She would depart and we would exchange winks.

Although I was very small, he would regale me with stories of his days searching for oil in Oklahoma, his brushes with Indians, his boyhood days in Chatham, his meetings with the political leaders of the state and nation. I shall never forget one morning when he sat up in bed and said, "My boy, come here." And as he did, he thrust out his right hand. "Shake hands," he ordered. I did. "I want you to remember that today you shook hands with the hand that shook hands with Abraham Lincoln." So the next time you see me and want to shake hands with the hand that shook hands with the hand that shook the hand of Abraham Lincoln, stick out your hand.

Burr Honed Aim at Kinderhook for Fatal Duel with Hamilton

As dawn broke on the morning of July 11, 1804, two angry rivals made their way to the heights of Weehawken, N.J., where—as the doggerel sung in many a home, as well as public places throughout the young United States, proclaimed:

Oh, Aaron Burr, Oh, Aaron Burr

What have you done?

You've gone and shot Great HAMILTON!

It was a shocking affair—two of the great men of the country engaged in mortal combat. One, the man who had been Washington's closest friend and advisor, as well as Secretary of the Treasury, was shot by Burr whose popularity was not as great as Hamiliton's but who had risen to the heights of Vice President of the United

States and had lost by only one vote from becoming Chief Executive of the nation.

Bitter feelings had existed between the two men, even as far back as the Revolution, when both served in the American Army. Many reasons have been given for the duel, and conjectures as to its cause have been offered ever since by historians. According to tradition, however, Burr had planned the confrontation for some time. It is known, too, that as a guest of Judge Peter Van Ness at his Kinderhook residence, then known as Kleerood, and later at Lindenwald, he practiced shooting with a pistol. Hours of practice with the weapon evidently bore him good results as he was able to hit and mortally wound Hamilton, but in turn, was not struck.

One of the two men selected by Burr to be his second at the Weehawken grounds was William (Billy) Van Ness of Kinderhook.

Kinderhook Seclusion

Almost immediately after the shots were fired by the two men, Van Ness came directly to Kinderhook and remained in temporary seclusion, as the feeling against Burr participants became more and more bitter with each passing day.

At the time over in Kinderhook there lived a young man known to his friends as "Matty" Van Buren, who was later to become the eighth president of the United States. He had only been admitted to the bar the year before at the Old Court House in Claverack, which still stands today.

His fame as a lawyer, despite the fact that he was only 21 years old, was rapidly growing throughout Columbia County. Billy Van Ness was fearful of an indictment as an accessory to the murder of Hamilton would be found against him and asked Van Buren to call at the Judge Van Ness home to discuss means of seeking bail should an indictment be handed down.

Van Buren, so far as is known, had no carriage at the moment, so he set out on foot for a three-mile walk to Kleerood. As he came up the circular driveway which led to the house, the young Kinderhook lawyer saw the judge with his back turned to the doorway at the main entrance. He was reading a newspaper and occupied this position as light was more favorable for his eyes.

Judge Van Ness was a man of strong and bitter dislikes and "Matty" had offended him by being a Democrat-Republican while the Van Ness families were strong Whigs. In fact, to the judge, anyone who leaned toward Jefferson was in the nature of a traitor to his country. As he heard Matty's steps on the driveway he turned about and saw who it was.

He again turned his back, thus preventing Van Buren from entering the house. The wily one who was later called "Fox of Kinderhook" was not to be outdone, so he seized the brass knocker at the top of the doors and beat loudly upon it. A smile came over the old judge's face; he apparently appreciated Matty's candor, and arising he went directly to the reception room but not a word did he speak to Van Buren.

Questions discussed

Billy Van Ness soon appeared at the door and with Van Buren went for a walk in the woods near Kinderhook Creek. In a small glen by the stream, they discussed questions which for the first time had brought the Kinderhook boy to the home of the aristocracy of the countryside.

In his autobiography, written in 1853, Mr. Van Buren related this incident and says that he made many alterations to Kleerood, whose name he changed to Lindenwald in 1841, but never did he touch the double doors which reminded him of his first visit there.

Billy was not indicted for murder, but he was disenfranchised. The bar later relented, and he was appointed a judge of the United

States District Court for the Southern District of New York by President James Madison.

Another tale

Then there is another tale, or one might better describe it as some of Lindenwald's folklore. It is about Aaron Burr, and while it sounds incredible, it was believed as gospel by many of the good people of Kinderhook a half century ago.

It seems that one hot summer's day a load of hay was being brought to the Lindenwald barns. Matty Van Buren had long been laid to rest in the Kinderhook cemetery and the property was owned by Adam E. Waggoner. A thunder shower was rolling up the valley of the Hudson and the men in the fields were fearful that the loads would be soaked. They hurried the teams along, but a black man who had been helping them was a bit slower because of lameness and lagged behind the others. He was out of earshot when a mass of swirling black clouds piled up over the Catskills and then swept down over the Kinderhook fields.

Suddenly, he heard a noise along the pathway he was walking and there beside him was a little man dressed in the costume of the early 1800s. The diminutive one bowed politely and then did a little jig. The black gentleman looked him over closely despite his sudden and startling appearance. "He was short, he had a pigtail in his hair, he had a prominent nose, and his clothes were elegant," he later recalled. At that moment a great clap of thunder shook the earth and the little visitor popped down a woodchuck hole, never again to be seen near Lindenwald. As the story was told and retold by Kinderhook housewives, all were in complete agreement that the elegantly dressed visitor was none other than "Burr who shot Hamilton."

Certainly Burr knew Lindenwald well during his life and better still did he know the famous Martin Van Buren who, in later years, was not adverse to calling the former vice president "his friend."

——♦——

Operation Overlord Anniversary

No stronger bond ever existed between America and Europe, 9/11 included, than 58 years ago on Saturday, June 6, 1944, when news of "Operation Overlord," the Allied invasion of France, was flashed to the free world. It was a day of prayer and tears. A devout and steady stream of humanity, from all walks of life, went to churches and synagogues to offer prayers for the safety of husbands, sons and brothers and the millions of men whose mission it was to drive the enemy from the Normandy coastline. Shortly after 7 P.M. General Dwight D. Eisenhower's terse message was received: "Allied forces in strength landed this morning to the coast of France."

D-Day at long last had become a reality.

In schools throughout Columbia County, pupils were urged to offer prayers for the men struggling at that hour in wave-swept assault boats heading toward the American landing areas at Omaha and Utah beaches. One of the best War Stamp sales was recorded that day in Chatham Elementary School. Announcement of the invasion launched a War Bond C Drive in Columbia County with a $1 million quota to buy famed Higgins' landing craft. On the streets of Valatie, Philmont, Hudson, Hillsdale and every other community, groups gathered around available radios to hear sporadic reports of the bloody beaches where the foot soldiers were landing.

On the 25th anniversary of the landing, June 6, 1959, Chatham observed D-Day with day-long activities including the planting of small oak saplings taken from an American battlefield near Metz, France. The saplings today are now mighty oaks standing before the

Chatham American Legion Post on Woodbridge Avenue and at the Mary E. Dardess Elementary School. At that time, I interviewed some of the local servicemen who had participated in the invasion. This is what I wrote:

At 12:30 P.M., a young paratrooper, his face blackened, stepped aboard a D-C 3 airplane. In his right pocket was $10 in invasion currency, a small American flag was sewn on his right sleeve and brown and green burlap were woven into his helmet netting for camouflage. Cpl. Robert C. Kellam, a trooper in the 506th Regt. 101 Airborne Division, was among the "Screaming Eagles" who would make an early jump to mark the landing zones for the main body—these were the "pathfinders" who hit the silk in the hours of darkness.

Kellam, an East Chatham resident, recalls, "We were dropped below Cherbourg with panels and markers to establish a DZ (drop zone) but we were scattered all over. I landed in a field, ducked into a nearby hedgerow, and immediately drew fire as we attempted to lay out markers. About dawn, two hours later, the main force of troopers landed. But it took us 34 days to fight our way out of Normandy."

Further to the east on the beaches, the great armada began spewing its cargo toward the German gun emplacements towering over Omaha Beach. Leading a platoon of the 117th Infantry, 30th Division, was 2nd Lt. Earl C. ("Pep") Smith of Chatham.

"It was frightening," Smith recalls, "the noise, the confusion, as we landed in support of the 29th Division which was pinned down on the beach. All that morning, I felt moved by some great force. I was wounded a few weeks later in the assault on St. Lo, and that put me out of action for good. I find myself remembering that day every year on June 6. I was just 19 years old at the time and it was a pretty big event in my life. It still is."

Another Chatham soldier, Anthony Cozzolino, a demolition expert with the 18th Regiment, 1st Infantry Division, landed from a small boat two hours before H-Hour (6 A.M.) to clear the beach of obstacles. "We didn't have that much to do as the frogmen had done a good job. The beach became real hot and we were pinned down the better part of a day and a half.

"The crossfire was murderous and it put the fear of God in you. I'd landed in North Africa and Sicily, but D-Day in France is one than I'll never forget—not that I haven't tried."

Donald Hanley, a burly former boxer and popular Chathamite, earned a citation for heroism as he laid Signal Corps communication wires along the beach for the embattled units.

Harold Gilbert of Ghent was aboard a Navy craft that poured shells into the enemy emplacement and Joseph Terraciano of Chatham was in the first wave of infantrymen that fought across Omaha Beach.

Former Chatham Mayor John A. Mesick also landed at H-Hour on Omaha Beach with the "Big Red One" division. In late June, Mesick was sent to a crossroads near St. Lo to mark a convoy route. The road came under heavy fire and the convoy dispersed, leaving Mesick alone. Separated from his unit, he was listed as "missing in action." Mesick stayed in the area for four days, then joined a platoon of the 3rd Infantry Division and fought with them all the way to Angers, 100 miles distant, before joining his unit 30 days later.

He received a citation awarding him the Croix de Guerre from the French government, but did not receive the medal until 25 years later at Chatham's special ceremonies on June 6, 1969.

This old scrivener made the landing on Utah Beach attached to the 4th Infantry Division. I was part of a small Franco-American unit of intelligence agents whose objective was a German school that was training stay-behind agents to commit acts of sabotage once the Allies landed. The school, a one-time farmhouse, was rubble when we arrived after a direct hit by the Army Air Corps.

As I look back this year on D-Day I shall take a moment to offer a prayer for those comrades who have answered the last roll call, including Bob Kellam, Tony Cozzolino, Don Hanley, Harold Gilbert and Joe Terraciano. At last word, Pep Smith is residing in Florida while Jack Mesick and yours truly still call the Town of Chatham home. If any of my readers are ever in New Orleans, the D-Day Museum in that city is a brilliant tribute to that historic day of long ago and should not be missed.

⇒◆⇐

The Day the War Ended

What were Columbia County residents doing 58 years ago this month? Well, to answer that question, let's look back at the time-yellowed pages of the *Chatham Courier* and the stories written by the editor, the late Carl West. The D-Day invasion of Normandy has taken place the year before, V-E Day in Europe had been celebrated in May 1945 but American battle forces were fighting the Japanese from island to island in the Pacific, and page after page of the *Courier* reported the day-to-day experiences of servicemen and women at home and abroad.

As of August 1, 1945, some 105 young men from Columbia County had given their lives in World War II, while 198 had been wounded and 23 were held prisoner by the Japanese. An additional 23 had been freed by Allied Forces from German prison camps. With most of the reporting staff in service, plus an acute shortage of newsprint, the *Courier* had been reduced to an average of eight pages a week, but those pages were filled with timely local news.

A front-page article gave the happy news that Pfc. Nelson Charron, 19, of Chatham, who had been reported missing in action in December 1944 and later a prisoner of war, was home once more.

Junior Red Cross girls from Chatham's seventh grade knitted six afghans which were sent to a New York City hospital for use by wounded veterans. Arlington Race of Spencertown, who penned a weekly column "The Roving Reporter" noted "long lines of people waiting in Chatham's Main St. for the IGA Store to open so they could purchase cigarettes. A short distance away there was another line waiting to buy chicken." He also noted, "old fashioned butter churns are popular again. With only margarine available, farm families are using churns to make their own butter."

The Berkshire Farm Agency in Chatham inserted a classified offering "Charming Old Chatham area eight-room house, 25 acres, view, roads, pond, springs. In excellent condition, $2,000. Easy terms available."

Chatham-area residents contributed three tons of used clothing to the United National Clothing Drive. Two hundred cartons were trucked to Hudson's National Guard Armory. Mrs. Richard Mason chaired the drive and drew a commendation from Mayor George Dennis for a "job well done."

The Joe Louis Club of Chatham met at the home of Mrs. William Kittle and set the date of a food sale for its Soldiers' Fund. Letters were read from men overseas thanking the club for cards, letters, and money they had received. Canaan residents had a field day as there was plenty of beef in town and no ration points. It all came about when a Holstein cow owned by Henry Nickles was killed by a B&A freight train. Canaanites, with carving knives in hand, flocked to the scene to obtain prime cuts—cinders and all.

Two Chatham brothers, who had not seen each other in a year, were united on the island of Guam in the Pacific. The servicemen are S/2c Thomas Diskin of the Navy and S/Sgt. James Diskin of the Army, sons of Mr. and Mrs. James Diskin of Chatham. A campaign to raise funds for the new Columbia Memorial Hospital was under way. At a meeting at the General Worth Hotel, in Hudson, it was announced that $400,000 had been pledged to date.

For those who had sufficient gasoline to get them to the Lebanon Valley, the Showboat featured the music of Cab Calloway and his orchestra. Dancers paid a 75 cent admission, except for servicemen and women, who were admitted free.

Chathamites strolling along Park Row stopped at Alvord's Drug Store to view a display of German war souvenirs, including guns, knives, uniforms, hats and medals that had been sent home by Sgt. Harry Mesick and Pfc. John Mesick of Chatham. The Mount Lebanon Shakers helped Sister Sadie Neal celebrate her 96th birthday. She had devoted 20 years to teaching school and, at the age of 70, helped issue the periodical *The Shaker*.

U.S. Internal Revenue Service agents paid a surprise visit to Chatham, checking cars that did not carry a $5 tax stamp displayed on the windshield. Some 10 summonses were issued. The *Courier* reported, "Chatham and its nearby hamlets went wild on Aug. 14 when Harry Truman announced Japan's surrender. Within a few minutes after the radio announced the news, sirens and blackout warning alarms sounded. Chatham Fire Dept. trucks, bedecked with flags and sirens sounding, drove through the village followed by more than 100 automobiles. Bars were jammed and extra bartenders and waitresses were pressed into service. Police Chief Harry Mack and Officer William Dalzell did excellent work in handling the traffic and merrymakers late into the night." Thus did World War II come to an end.

———✦◦◦✦———

Remember Pearl Harbor—If You Do, You're Old

December 7, the day that Franklin Roosevelt said would live in infamy, has usually rated a whole paragraph in most of the papers and received short shrift on radio and TV. "Remember Pearl Harbor" is almost forgotten now, except among the dwindling few whose lives were changed forever on that beautiful warm Sunday in another world. Now, on the 50th anniversary of the Japanese attack, memories come flooding back for those of us who can recall December 7, 1941. On August 11, 1941, I had gone to New York City to enlist in the United States Army, raised my right hand and swore to "defend this nation against all enemies, both foreign and domestic."

Draft Board No. 312 had been breathing down the neck of every young man in Chatham who had a pulse beat. Now, classified 1A, which signified I was wanted by Uncle Sam, I arrived at 59 Whitehall St. in downtown Manhattan. With eight years of French both at Chatham High and Union College, and an additional four years of college German, I applied for service in the United States Military Intelligence Division.

Standing in line with other recruits, I heard my name called and before my army career was 20 minutes old, I was handed a document directing me to report to Fort Jay, Headquarters, 2nd Service Command. I had not the foggiest idea where Fort Jay might be, but you soon learn in the army to carry out orders without asking questions. My enlistment papers further directed me to report to the 120th Service Unit. The ferry ride from the Battery to the island provided a spectacular view of lower Manhattan's skyline, and 20 minutes later I was at my new home away from home.

But there was something strange about this bastion of defense. Except for the Military Police, few, if any of the men, young or old, were in uniform. Walking down a tree-lined street past handsome Georgian-style, brick buildings, I felt this was a college campus not an army post.

My barracks were still several hundred yards away and in the warmth of the August sun, I heard muffled applause, click-click-click, kah-lumph, kah-lumph, kah-lumph, click-click-click, muffled applause, there on a magnificent field was a polo game observed by handsomely dressed men and women. Seated under green and white umbrellas, they were quaffing cool libations served by young men wearing white gloves and jackets. This is the army?

The day prior to Pearl Harbor on Governor's Island was lively and animated. I was assigned to the G-2 (Intelligence) Section and although my rank was a private and my pay was $21 a month, I carried the imposing designation of Special Agent in the United States Army Counterintelligence Corps (CIC). I believe I am one of a handful of people who took their basic training on Governors Island. Unlike other GIs who slogged through the red clay of Georgia or sweated in Louisiana swamps, my training would have done credit to a Harvard classroom.

There were perhaps eight of us who met four afternoons a week with Master Sergeant Thaddeus Dombloski, USA, who had served as a machine gunner with the 4th Infantry Division in France during World War I. M/Sgt. Dombloski would take us out into the "field"—the polo field—where, wearing flat, dish-type World War I helmets, fatigues and puttees that laced up the side, we would do close-order drill, stamping down the divots gouged out by the polo ponies.

We field stripped the Colt .45 pistol, the Springfield rifle (the Garrand M-1 of the army's arsenal of weapons which seemingly had been made available to every soldier except those of us in the 120th service Unit).

But M/Sgt. Dombloski did have one weapon that was his pride and joy—a Browning water-cooled machine gun—a holdover from the Great War, but in the intervening years, the hose connecting the water can to the barrel had been lost. It was great to look at, to assemble and disassemble, but as a killer it was impotent. Basic training lasted for three months and it was now mid-November. As winter approached and the cold intensified, so did the Governors Island social whirl.

The officers and their ladies, with the polo season over, were now enjoying a succession of parties and dances both on the island and in Manhattan. Life for enlisted personnel was not that bad either. New York and New Yorkers went all out to welcome and entertain members of the Armed Forces. At the USO headquarters in the Hotel Astor there were free tickets not only for movies but the best Broadway shows. Nightclubs and restaurants offered special rates for servicemen and women, as did hotels. You wouldn't buy a drink at a bar if you were in uniform; other bar patrons bought them for you.

November drifted into December and with each passing day, the tenseness increased. The G-2 section got the bulk of its news from Associated Press and United States wire services, and their machines chattered out history 24 hours a day. The U.S. destroyer *Reuben James* was sunk in the North Atlantic, as well as several other destroyers sent to Great Britain on a lend-lease basis. Japanese diplomats were in Washington on a "peace mission," and each day the nation waited anxiously to hear the outcome of their deliberations; the second hand on peace was winding down.

Sunday, December 7, 1941, was chilly, cloudy and windy in New York City. As it happened, I pulled duty that Sabbath in the G-2 section and fretfully envied my friends who had gone to a New York

Giants football game. Just another dull day until 5 P.M. when my relief would arrive. It was our duty in the G-2 section to make perfunctory calls to the Brooklyn Navy Yard, the Coast Guard, Mitchell Field, Fort Totten and the New York Police Dept. to double check any incidents that might hint of sabotage or breach of army security.

The wire service machines chattered endlessly and then they stopped. The bells on the AP unit began to reverberate and were joined moments later by the UP machine. Then the letters tapped out with chilling intensity. FLASH . . . JAPANESE AIRCRAFT ATTACKED THE UNITED STATES NAVAL BASE AT PEARL HARBOR AT 7:45 A.M. PACIFIC TIME. STAND BY . . .

My quiet Sunday changed instantaneously into gut-wrenching spasms of anxiety. There was a "secret" list of personnel to be notified in the event of an "extreme emergency," beginning with the commanding general, my commanding officer and other duty officers on the island. Within an hour, Governors Island was on full alert, and what was almost amusing, everyone reported for duty in uniform. An announcement was made at the Giants' game for all armed forces personnel to "return to their bases immediately." It wasn't long before the G-2 section was completely staffed and in full operation.

I stayed on duty until 10 P.M., then took the subway uptown to Grand Central. Few people were in the streets and the city was almost calm. In restaurants, people clustered about radios to hear the fearful news coming from the Pacific. Trucks with loudspeakers moved through Midtown ordering service personnel to report to their units. New York City was preparing to take sword in hand.

Four days later on December 11, a message was sent from a Signal Corps outpost at the tip of Long Island to the G-2 section. "Can you confirm that a flight of enemy aircraft is one hour's flying time from New York City?" Somewhere along the line at Mitchell Field or Fort Totten the question was twisted into a positive statement, that enemy bombers were approaching New York. The army notified city officials. Air raid sirens wailed. Crews tested antiaircraft guns atop tall buildings. People leaned out windows to get a glimpse of the incoming flight. The afternoon was clear and bright. How would we defend ourselves? The answer came moments later when from the east came the sound of a single airplane, an army bi-plane with blue fuselage and yellow wings. It circled bravely, alone, criss-crossing Manhattan waiting to fire at will against the Axis invaders.

I glanced up at the great parapets of Fort Jay which loom over Governors Island. There on the fortification silhouetted against the sky, was M/Sgt. Thaddeus Dombloski wearing his WWI helmet, bands of machine gun rounds slung over his shoulder, his .30 calibre water-cooled Browning machine gun pointed skyward—without the connecting hose. A half hour later, the confusion was corrected. There was no air raid, but New Yorkers felt a wee bit braver for the ordeal they had undergone.

War had come at last to the city of idle dreams and Britain no longer stood alone.

COUNTRY LIFE

The Autumnal Pleasure of Burning Leaves

About this time of year the nose wrinkles up—"sniffing the air inter-rogatively" as Henry James once put it—trying to remember the smell of burning leaves. When was it—years ago now—that the bon-fires were first forbidden? Cigarette smokers still fill a few bars and restaurants with their clouds. Carbon monoxide still floats over the highways at commuter hours. But we have saved dear old Columbia County from air pollution by banning the burning of leaves. Well, to be perfectly fair, we've saved the fire department from a few trips, too. Still, something has gone out of life that permitted us our small ritual to signal the change of seasons. Stuffing a wad of murky leaves into a plastic bag doesn't do it. Neither does raking leaves into fur-rows along the street where they will be inhaled by a giant automo-tive vacuum. If the smell of leaves was a pollutant, it certainly was the most pungent of pollutants—outdoor incense.

The wrinkled-up nose became an expert at distinguishing aro-matic varieties. There was the oak fragrance, the maple smell, the lovely mixed-with-pine-needles aroma. As the last autumnal burn-ings took place, these perfumes could fill a whole neighborhood. Today's youngsters have been denied one of the few chores all of us enjoyed in our youth—raking and burning leaves. Raking is boring, but igniting the big pile that had carefully been gathered downwind of any structures (you'd surely catch hell if you burned down the house or even the chicken coop) and then touching a match to the multi-colored mass . . . I still have fond recollections of walking home on a late November afternoon from Prof. Armitage's School for Young Men and Women on Woodbridge Ave., scuffing the little piles of leaves and savoring the burned woody fragrance in a mellow stillness I shall never forget. Time drifted in slow motion, like the last falling leaf.

In the 1930s, Chatham's Payn Avenue was covered with a bower of branches reaching up and outward from columns of elm trees that marched down each side of the thoroughfare. And each autumn these elms released a zillion leaves. I shall always recall one glorious night when a full moon brightened the countryside, illuminating the pile of leaves that had accumulated in the street. My neighbor Charles (Chick) Rivenburgh, who had also spent the late afternoon raking, emerged from his house and said with authority, "There's not a breath of wind tonight, let's get to burning." Oh, glorious words! Oh, glorious night!

The ceremony of burning turned the most agitated overachiever into a serene philosopher. It was humanly impossible to do anything but become a spectator—lean on the rake, nostrils pleasantly nipped by curls of smoke, and watch a pile of leaves reduce itself from shooting flames to a bed of glowing sparks—like the last tint of a gorgeous sunset. Only the reds and yellows of a bonfire could do justice to the colors of the leaves consumed.

The black plastic bag with the little twist at the neck hustles the leaves out of town and disposes of them, like a public nuisance. The bonfire lent a little honor and festivity to the occasion. And late autumn is a season that needs all the brightness, all the warmth, all the pungency, all the parties it can get. Even lyric poets mope and mutter about "the sere and yellow leaf" not to mention "the bare, ruined choirs of trees those leaves have just abandoned." Emily Dickinson, an underachieved New Englander, saw autumn as "prosaic days/A little side of the snow/and that side of the haze."

The bonfire of leaves put the poetry back in autumn. As the earth turned brown and white, here was one last blaze of primary colors—one final salute of fireworks to remember what had been and what would be again after the season of cold storage. I well recall Miss Margaret Weiss, my high school art teacher, describing the Impressionism of Claude Monet. With admiration and precision she described Monet's trees as "not really a tree, but just something surrounded by beautiful color."

Bonfires turned ordinary dead leaves into "something surrounded by beautiful color"—an act of Impressionism, an act of life. Are all fires finally signal fires? In the name of public safety, in the name of environmentalism we can do without these ancient comforts—these primeval invitations of the human community to come huddle. But perhaps one day a year, if everybody gave up smoking and driving for eight hours, we could afford as tradeoff one magnificent leaf fire in the center of town—just to bring back all those nice caveman memories.

——>◆<——

The Blessing

The estate on White Bridge Road near Old Chatham was called "Banbury Cross" and its owner was a lady of great elegance, refinement, self-assurance and the mistress of a splendid pack of bassets.

Each of the hounds was named for some precious jewel. They were known as "the Bijoux Bassets of Banbury Cross," and when they traveled to meets some distance away they rode in their own trailer. This conveyance was painted a deep ashes of roses and decorated with doves in flight. It was called "the Bijoux Bassinet."

Often she would admire them as they lunged against the wire of the pens, howling with excitement. On one of these occasions, she composed a little verse: "Darling little bassets with your shiny, twinkling facets."

The interior of her home was a replica of one of Madame du Barry's little pleasure palaces in France.

There were dovecotes placed among the lilacs. "My little Versailles," she called it as she watched a flock of fantail pigeons concern themselves with lovemaking. Haughty white peacocks proudly traipsed their snowy trains across the perfectly clipped lawns. Just off the rear of the house was a fenced-in courtyard where tiny walks led to a pool and a statue of Jupiter and Prosperine. Water bubbled in the pool and the pigeons would sweep into the crab apple trees in the courtyard before wheeling down into the fountain during midday's heat. Throughout the house were cages of turtle doves. "Tortues," she called them, and they mourned and cooed all day. The screeching of the peacocks, the cooing of the doves and pigeons and the baying of the bassets all made a bright background for their lively and energetic mistress.

She was a splendid horsewoman and the only lady a half century ago who rode side saddle with the Old Chatham Hunt and the Carroll Hounds. Having an unusual and excellent seat, she was, at times, the envy of the more sedate lady riders. She wore a top hat, from which was draped a veil which covered her handsome features, a perfectly tailored black jacket, a brilliant white stock and pin nestled under her chin and a long, black skirt covered her brilliantly polished boots. She was a fearless rider who had spent many autumns as a guest of hunts in Ireland, where she became famous for clearing the most formidable stone walls and ditches. She loved to ride flat out at the greatest speed and to the chagrin of the MFH, she was often ahead of the hounds.

The late Blanchard Rand, MFH of the Old Chatham, recalled a Saturday hunt where, "We were going away on a big red fox and when I looked again I saw the fox was running close behind the heels of her mare."

Though still full of *joie de vivre,* she had given up the pursuit of Reynard to the following of the hare or "cottontail," as it was known by the villagers. In this sport she was as adept as she was in fox hunting. When the Bijoux Bassets went afield, she could be seen climbing walls, squeezing through barbed wire and often wading knee deep across the slippery stones of a stream. Henry, her faithful kennelman and groom, would follow a pace or so to her rear, while short-winded guests in the field would taggle on behind the pack as best they could.

As St. Hubert's Day came around, it was customary to have the pack blessed on this day of the saint, who guides hunters in the field. The tradition probably started at the royal court of some European monarch, and a nearby local priest was wheedled and cajoled into performing the ancient ceremony.

"How can a pack of hounds be properly blessed without holy water?" she peeped when it was suggested the dominie of the Old Chatham Methodist Church might do just as well. Not at all, and it would be a priest who, after all, could use the check, a brace of guinea hens or muscovy ducks and a bottle of Moët et Chandon Champagne to wash down the offering.

Father O'Reilly deeply appreciated the check and whatever fowl she might give him. "Someday she'll make a mistake and give me a pair of those screamin' paycocks and that'll be it," he told his housekeeper. Each year she would call and implore him to bless the hounds, the hunt staff and the field, and his response was always the same. His real ordeal with the blessing of the pack stemmed from the fact that his dear mother in Ireland had once had her wits scared out of her by a pack of gigantic stag hounds. This inherent fear of his mother's was also his and the hackles on his back would rise at the sight of any dog, but a whole pack of 'em—Holy Mother! Pleasantly she would chide the good man of the cloth about the church's attitude toward superstitions, followed by a discourse on old wives' tales. He inevitably, if reluctantly, would agree to come.

On this particular morning, the lady arose from her canopied Louis XIV bed, dressed and went directly to the kennels. The hounds lunged against the wire and howled their welcome. The salute pleased her but in the gray light of the half-spent dawn, she sensed that something was amiss. Entering a small outbuilding near the kennel that was used for cutting up horse meat and preparing the hounds' food, she peered into the half darkness.

To her horror and consternation, she saw Henry, the groom-kennelman, "hanging by the neck from an overhead beam," as she related later. His face was the shade of hardened putty and gasping, gurgling noises emanated from his throat. Grabbing a huge knife that was used to hack up horse meat, she jumped up on the tub that Henry had stood on before kicking it away. With one swift stroke or two of the knife, she severed the rope. Henry fell from the rafter, sounds like water going down a clogged drain of a bathtub issuing from his open mouth.

Helping him to his feet and shaking him violently, she shouted, "How dare you do such a thing? St. Hubert's Day. The blessing. The guests. The press. Photographers. Father O'Reilly. I repeat, how dare you do such a thing on this particular day? Go in the house and take a drink of something. Anything. We'll discuss the matter later." And she sent him on his way with a well placed foot on his posterior.

Massaging his throat, he staggered dizzily into the kitchen only to hear her voice again. "Remember about Pearl, Opal and Amethyst. They're in heat; don't let them out with the other hounds. Remember last year? Remember, lout, goon!" After a quick shower, the lady changed into her hunting livery, a dusty rose jacket with black velvet piping at the collar, a black velvet visored cap (embroidered with B.B.) and a doeskin skirt over knee-length dusty rose socks and well-worn hunting shoes that she had purchased at Swayne & Adney in London. As she went through the hall, she picked up her riding crop and silver hunting horn. Passing though the kitchen, she gave a few cursory orders to the staff who were preparing the breakfast that would be served after the hunt.

Presently, the sound of approaching cars could be heard rattling over the wooden bridge at the foot of the hill. The lady greeted her guests; there was twittering and talk and some gallantry from the men who bowed and kissed her extended hand. Reporters with cameras over their shoulders arrived as did Father O'Reilly, looking concerned and quite red of face. Over his long black cassock, he wore a white surplice and carried a missal in one hand and the aspergillum in the other.

The whippers-in cracked whips and shouted until the pack was brought to the front steps of the house where, over the doorway, was a handsomely carved outline of a hound's head and a French hunting horn. Cameras clicked. Beryl and Garnet howled dismally. Father O'Reilly opened his book, hastily completed the prayer and lifting the aspergillum, sprinkled the pack with holy water. Diamond at this point nudged the hem of the Father's cassock, causing the good man to levitate two steps higher.

The lady introduced the members of her staff, welcomed the field and made known that a collation would be served when they returned. Notes from her silver horn danced in the air and the pack moved out, but not far. From the corner of the house came sounds of fury and muffled snarls. Henry had forgotten to hook the gate. Pearl, Amethyst and Opal had rejoined the pack in full bloom and the males went savagely at each others' throats in an attempt to be the first to deflower the maidens. Whips snapped, but the pack joined in a real free-for-all, guests fled, and the lady raised her horn again and blew lustily. The three bitches were returned to the kennel.

Order was now restored and the pack moved across the bridge toward the Benedict farm for the morning hunt. Father O'Reilly, who had agreed to stay for the breakfast but declined to follow the hounds, quickly found the bar and swallowed three fingers of Scotch. As the Bijoux Bassets went screaming after a cottontail, Father O'Reilly looked out the window and made an absolute vow to himself—"This is most definitely the last time, so help me."

=—◆—=

Storm Is Gone, But Memories Linger On

The media called it "the storm of the century," but to a few of us old graybeards, it was just another good winter storm, quite reminiscent of other blizzards we experienced in winters past. Perhaps we were made of tougher stuff back in the 1920s and '30s. No school closing for us. As youngsters we didn't sit by the radio or TV to wait anxiously to see if our school was closed.

We had only one radio station in those days, good old WGY in Schenectady, and that didn't broadcast school closings. Boob tubes were still years away from becoming operative in the family living room.

There were no school cafeterias. You walked through the snow to school in the morning, walked home at the end of day. If the weather was very stormy, Mother packed a brown-bag lunch, and those of us in grade school would gather in an empty room on the ground floor of the Woodbridge Ave. school in Chatham. I shall never forget the redolent effluvium that arose from wet socks, manure-laden boots, peanut butter sandwiches and unwashed bodies. There were no "snow days." I recall only one incident that closed the Chatham School in winter and that was when a furnace blew up.

It was rather a glorious day in my life. I had forged through waist-deep snow from Payn Avenue "backlots" to Church Street, then down Woodbridge where a horse-drawn plow had cleared the sidewalk. Just as I reached the Woodbridge Ave. crossing, the whistle on the Chatham Shirt Factory on Church Street split the morning air with a continuing number of sharp blasts. This was Chatham's fire alarm. It was a dreaded sound when heard at night, but in the daylight it only created excitement among those of us trudging to 8 A.M. classes.

From up Kinderhook Street way we could hear the sound of a siren and we broke into a full run when we saw Ocean Fire Co. No. 1 pull up at the back of the school. Smoke was pouring out of a basement door and out of it came the Reverend Andrew Pinkerton, a school custodian. His face was covered with soot and he was coughing heavily.

"It's the furnace," he gasped. The thought of old Chatham High School going up in flames was an exhilarating yet awesome thought.

The firemen rammed their engine through the snow and disappeared into the basement with a hose line. Moments later they emerged. The fire was out. Then Prof. A. Wesley Armitage, the school principal, announced that, because there would be no heat in school, classes were dismissed. O, glorious day!

It was back home to get out the Flexible Flyer, tramp down a track on Browning's Hill and build a jump from which we could "bellywop" into space. It was a wonderful afternoon and still lives in my memory because of the singular happenstance of having no school on a weekday. The Reverend Pinkerton got the furnace started and it was back to the old routine the next day, come hell or high snow.

As the snow piled up on the weekend and traffic came almost to a stop, I made one last dash to the Old Chatham Country Store for a few items to carry us through the storm.

The store parking lot, usually filled to capacity, harbored only three vehicles—all of them Volvos—and therein lies a tale.

I am convinced that Volvo drivers like to pretend that there are no other cars on the road. Blizzards mean nothing to them. They are surrounded by eight tons of metal and an impenetrable aura of smugness. The Volvo owners were complacently sipping coffee in the store's restaurant, completely oblivious to the raging storm outside. I was in a state of panic to get home, but not they.

Volvo drivers go out in any kind of weather. They drive in whatever lane they choose, at whatever speed they choose. Maybe they drive in two lanes simultaneously, maybe they drive right next to the curb where cyclists travel and children play; c'est la bloody vie, big boy. The world owes them space. This is the Volvo attitude.

I ask you to make this simple experiment.

For one week, as you motor about the highways and byways of this great bioregion, note every instance of bad driving that you encounter. Do not curse and scream, although you are free to do that as well. Note carefully the make of vehicle engaged in the bad driving. At the end of the week tally the results.

I'd be willing to wager that I could predict the top four places on your list, together with a list of the most common driving errors attributable to each vehicle.

    1.   Volvo. Oh, look, it's the Queen Mother out for a drive. Her little babies are on board; her dog, Ginger, and $200 worth of groceries. She's entering the Thruway. She's going 13

miles an hour. Oops, was that an accident behind her? There's her off-ramp. But now she's going 75 in the left lane. No problem! She gives the commoner a gracious wave.

2. Any General Motors car manufactured before 1970. Traffic laws are for fools. He has 385 horses under his hood and power steering that responds to the touch of a finger, if it responds at all. Zow, whooooooosh, ratatata, hatatatata. Brakes pull badly to the left; tail pipe dances like a sailor; breathalyzer a mere formality. Driver still remembers Andrew Dice Clay.

3. Mercedes-Benz. Diesel powered for maximum choke effect. The driver listens to his tape while fiddling with car fax; checks the road only occasionally. Personalized license plate. Drives too fast except when he's on car phone, then he drives too slow. Coat carefully hung up in back seat. Probably owns slum property. Changes lanes incessantly in traffic jams, searching for extra edge.

4. VW Bus. Bumper stickers promote solar power and discredited Central American revolutionary groups. Crystal hangs from rear-view mirror; paisley fabric over rear window. Wildly under-powered; sometimes cannot get across intersection from a standing start before light changes. Karmic route-planning techniques. Will move sideways in whirl; needs all four lanes to cross Rip Van Winkle Bridge.

You already know I'm right. Even Volvo drivers know I'm right. They try to improve, but something happens when they get behind the wheel. The movie of those crash tests plays over and over in their brain. That's the official Volvo slogan; I'm safe no matter what—even in the "storm of the century"—watch out, America.

Bottoming out: I kept my Christmas tree and used it as a bird feeder. The weekend storm brought flocks of usual visitors—

cardinals, finches, chickadees, tufted titmice, white throat and tree sparrows, juncos, *ad infinitum,* but Saturday midday as the snow was swirling and dancing about my Yule tree, I spotted a fat little unfamiliar figure. Lo and behold a Carolina wren. Perhaps she was blown northward in the storm; but, be that as it may, I like to think of her as an early migrant. Can spring and daffodils and peepers and skunk cabbage be far behind?

———◆———

Spring Tonics

Lady April has not been letting down her rain-drenched hair, nor has she been laughing her girlish laughter as the poets picture her. But a bluebird has been bugling its cheerful song and inspecting our long-vacant bluebird house. It's for rent, for free! Three pairs of robins have stopped their feuding and courtship and staked their claims for home sites. They are excellent masons. Already the mud foundations and sidewalls of a nest are evident in the grape arbor and soon will be ready for occupancy.

Spring tonics: Who recalls a bitter brew that came in a brown bottle with a yellow label? It was called Atwoods Bitters and it was supposed to do you good—come spring. At the same time, a large earthenware bowl was placed on the kitchen table. This held a ghastly looking elixir of sulphur and molasses. Everyone helped himself—with the same spoon. A daily dollop was supposed to tune up your "cistern" (system) and purify the blood.

Seymour's Drug Store in Chatham carried a supply of "slippery ellum" (elm) bark for coughs, colds and other pulmonary maladies. It had the consistency of diluted wall paste and certainly was not as palatable. Another spring favorite was Dent de Lion, from the out-lines of the leaves, as the French call them. A dandelion, by any name, is a healthy spring dish. They are cheap, too, since they cost nothing but the effort of picking.

A new suggestion for preparing them: Take one and a half pounds of fresh young greens and wash well. Remove tough, outer leaves. Boil in salted water for 30 minutes. Drain thoroughly and chop coarsely. Melt two tablespoons of butter, add tablespoon of flour. Mix the "roux" until it is smooth. Add one-half cup beef consommé. Stir. Add salt, pepper to taste. When sauce is smooth, add dandelions and reheat. Serves four.

We stopped at the Old Chatham Country Store the other day and it pleased us to note that they still carry an ample supply of "chawin' terbaccer." Seeing the various brands, it brought to mind one from our boyhood—"Red Hook," by name. It came in a generous-sized package, Prussian blue in color. Chawers as well as smokers liked it. An ancient lady, who lives on Seven Bridges Road, smoked the lethal tobacco for a pain in her side. George Luks, the noted artist, painted her, a pipe clenched in her mouth and a white rooster perched on her shoulder. *The Widow of Seven Bridges Road* hangs in the Whitney in New York City.

I recall the tip of the widow's pipe was well wrapped in store cord since she had long ago lost her teeth. No one saw her in the act of drawing this cure into her lungs. She would totter out to the "Ladies Walk" at the edge of the woods near her home. Eventually, clouds of smoke would pour from the only window of the tiny building—along with swarms of wasps.

Strangers, on passing, would come to a sudden halt and shout, "Hi! Your outhouse is on fire." Whoever happened to go to the front door would say in an offhand manner, "Oh, that's only Grandma taking a little comfort with her Red Hook."

Bottoming out: The too-eager gardener should heed the oldtime farmer's advice. Wait until the young leaves on the maples are the size of a kitten's ear before planting anything. Peas and parsley excepted.

——=>·•·<=——

Tally Ho!
Foxhunters Mark 44th Year of Pursuing Wily Reynard Over the Countryside

The plaintive notes of a copper horn followed by the joyous music of a pack of hounds in full chase echo across the Old Chatham frost-filled fields these October morns, signaling the 44th anniversary of a time-honored sport of fox hunting in Columbia County. At one time there were nearly a dozen registered foxhunting packs in New York State, but with ever-increasing networks of roads and the gradual expansion of urban areas, foxhunting country has been reduced to a minimum—particularly on Long Island and in Westchester County where a number of packs once flourished. In addition, there are fewer farms and, where horses, riders and hounds once coursed over open countryside, they now have cut paths through second-growth alder that has sprung up from long unplanted fields.

Dutchess County still has two hunts—the Millbrook and Rambout—but here, too, a rapidly expanding population is gradually absorbing the few remaining acres of good, open hunting ground. This leaves Columbia as one of the best, if not the best foxhunting countryside in the northeastern United States, rivaled only by Virginia's rolling hills and fields.

Foxhunting in Columbia County dates back to 1926, when a small group of horsemen, sparked by the late Capt. Sidney R. Smith of Canaan and the late W. Gordon Cox of New Lebanon, established the Lebanon Valley Hunt. Capt. Smith had gained hunting experience in England and he approached the late Mr. Cox of New Lebanon on the subject. Mr. Cox had not only become a hunt member, but an almost legendary figure as one of the greatest whippers-in in the history of American foxhunting.

Col. William Adams of Canaan was also an early member and president of the club.

The George Tilden residence at New Lebanon became the hunt's clubhouse, and stables and kennels were readied for what was expected to be many, many years of happy hunting. As time wore on, however, the country proved too hilly for good riding and the ever-expanding forests presented too much of an obstacle to horses and riders. It was decided then and there to seek new country.

In 1929 Mr. Cox and Blanchard Rand, a prominent horseman and polo player who resided in Salisbury, Conn., were invited by the late Mr. Wilson Powell of Old Chatham to look over what was known as the Squire Hammond Property as the possible site of a new clubhouse.

The house and country were ideal and the Lebanon Valley Hunt moved to its new location where it became the Old Chatham Hunt. The Hammond House, now the B. L. Rosenthal residence, was remodeled for a professional huntsman, a 40-stall hunting stable was reconstructed from existing barns, locker rooms were provided for professional whips and grooms, and kennels were constructed for the pack of foxhounds. The late Blanchard Rand became master of the Old Chatham Hunt.

Mr. John Manning from Albany joined the ranks and his generosity made it possible to remodel the clubhouse and build a small cottage for the huntsmen. With 60 riders frequently in the field on a good October morning, some of the nation's prominent families, the Roosevelts of Hyde Park, the Saltonstalls of Boston and the Astors of Long Island rode with the Old Chatham Hunt. During the season the Saltonstalls rented a home near New Concord to be close by. Foxes were plentiful, fields were open and long runs were experienced all the way from Canaan Center to Malden Bridge with not a major highway to cross.

For one year the late W. Gordon Cox and the late Chester Braman ran the hunt as a committee of two, Mr. Rand having retired with the approaching war. Gordon Cox refused to continue because of increasing urgency of business. Chester Braman continued for one year as MFH. A number of young men who had ridden with the hunt were entering service, and with gasoline and meat rationing it became impossible to transport horses and feed a pack of foxhounds. The Old Chatham Hunt became a victim of World War II.

The late artist John Carroll at this time decided to take the Old Chatham hounds to his farm near East Chatham. The country formerly hunted by the O. C. H. was called the New Britain Country. The Carroll Hounds were organized. The then Mrs. W. Gordon Cox became joint master with John Carroll, who had built up his country and revived interest. Captain Smith also joined the ranks there for a short period. Mr. Carroll having retired in 1954, the Old Chatham Hunt was reorganized. A clubhouse was established at Mr. and Mrs. Cox's Antinore Farm at Old Chatham. A number of outside activities were established and the Hunt acquired a pack of beagles, thus being the first hunt to have both foxhounds and beagles.

Mrs. Cox and Capt. Smith were joint masters. Mr. Hugh Johnston and Orlan Johnson were present at the reorganization as were Mr. Gordon Cox, Mr. John Williams and the late Everett Gidley. Captain Smith retired as joint master after a year and Everett Gidley joined Mrs. Cox as joint master. Captain Smith became honorary secretary, a post which he held admirably for ten years. William F. Shaw succeeded Everett Gidley as joint master with Mrs. Gordon Cox. The hunt flourished for many years, Mr. Shaw also acting as honorary huntsman, a difficult task he succeeded in doing brilliantly. Up to this time the hunt had always has a professional huntsman. Gordon "Pete" Cox became joint master with Mr. Shaw replacing his mother, Mrs. John S. Williams, who retired in 1968.

At the present time, Mr. Shaw having retired in 1969, Pete Cox is carrying on as proficiently as his father before him and a new staff has taken over the duties. Mr. Ronald Jeacon, field master, is hunt secretary treasurer. Honorary whips are Mr. Edgar Behrens, Mr. Arthur Heins, Mrs. William White, Miss Gail Behrens and Mr. William Morin, ensuring that gates are kept closed, that fencing is repaired when needed and that riders keep off freshly planted lands.

Preparing for foxhunting begins in September when a cubbing season gets underway. This is designed to break up the dens of fox cubs and scatter the young dogs and vixens about the countryside. The first week in October the hunt actually begins with the traditional blessing of the hounds and riders in the Old Chatham village square. A hunt breakfast for those who have spent a chilly morning in the open usually follows at the home of a hunt member.

Hunting will continue until the ground freezes so hard as to make footing for horses dangerous. However, until that time, the Old Chatham hills will ring to the melodic sounds of the huntsman's horn and hounds. Reynard usually manages to outwit his pursuers, even resorting to dashing through Old Chatham's village square as he did a few years ago, and those who saw the wily old fellow swore he had a smile on his face as if enjoying the pursuit by baying hounds and hurrying horsemen.

Country Noises

To the untrained ear of the city dweller, the first year of living in the country can be quite a challenge. Having spent most of their lives amidst the din and clatter of some large urban sprawl, they find acoustical adjustment difficult. Often, after a nerve-wracking year, they sell their newly acquired country home and return to their more familiar sounds.

An empty garbage can, flung hard to the pavement, is music to their ears. At least they know what makes the din. Recently, we met a couple who had resided since childhood in New York City. Reaching retirement age, they decided to get away from it all. So, they drove up the Taconic Parkway, met with local realtors and eventually bought a home in what is known locally as the Macedonia section of Austerlitz. Adjusting to this pastoral life on a dirt road in a densely wooded area almost ruined their nervous systems, not to mention their dispositions.

A swamp-load of peepers (music to a countryman's ears) can bring wonderment and sleepless nights to the urbanite when first he hears their early spring chorus.

"Them's peepers," the mailman tells the city person. "Harmless as a fly."

Sitting by an open window on a sizzling summer night, hoping to be soothed by some fragrant breeze, the stillness can be shattered by a raunchy June bug as it hurls itself with violence against a door screen. Trooper Earl Hanchett, who served the New Lebanon State Police Station for many years, fondly recalls an ex-urbanite who purchased a home on Gale Hill Road. Late one summer's evening, the high-strung homeowner called the troopers on the phone screaming he was being fired at by an assailant—WHAM! . . . the assault went on, even after putting out the lights. Arriving at the house, Trooper Hanchett found a sweat-soaked "2-1-2" standing in the kitchen while an enormous June bug dive bombed the screen door.

A family of chimney swallows, clawing and chattering while trying to get a toehold and failing, come swooshing down the chimney and after a moment, go whirling upward again.

After one has fallen into a fitful sleep the welcome light of dawn trips through the window, but peace doesn't accompany the brightening day. In short time the swallows discover their stomachs are empty and throbbing. They set up a chatter that would dim the noise of a flock of locusts. Mama and Papa Swallow dart in and out of the chimney with morsels of food while the little tots chatter with content.

Red squirrels playing bocce with black walnuts on the attic floor quickly end the delights of country living. Country boys can also explode visions of bucolic happiness with their ghastly Halloween tricks. Perhaps the best I can recall as a youth involved a couple from Yonkers who purchased a home on Chatham's Payn Avenue. It was mid-October when they moved in and they became a ready target for pranksters at Halloween.

Several scoundrels, including yours truly, peeked in their living room window and saw they were comfortably seated listening to Amos and Andy on their Atwater Kent radio. At this point, we inserted a nail into the aperture between the window and the sill. A strong fish line was tied to the nail head and stretched to a safe distance behind a tree. We then applied resin to the line and instantly the living room was filled with screams and echoes like a demented violinist playing his favorite cadenza. The poor man levitated out of his chair and his wife let out a shrill screech. We didn't hang around to see further results of our skullduggery, but it's almost certain the poor couple didn't sleep well that night, probably thinking their newly acquired house was haunted.

Let us return for a moment to those people who bought the house in Austerlitz. There they are sitting on the edge of their bed, clinging to each other wide-eyed and frantic. They vow to return to their Manhattan digs. "It may be small, but at least it's quiet," she declares and he, shakingly, agrees.

The Hornin'

As the years go by and after penning these columns for more than four decades, I can well recall what the late Anna Rundell, Spencertown's never-to-be-forgotten correspondent, once told me. Arriving at the *Courier* office, she looked heavenward and said with a sigh, "After penning thousands and thousands of words, I'm just about writ out!" I often feel the same way and realize that I'm probably recalling once too often the subjects I've written about in the past.

In a recent copy of this newspaper, however, there appeared a small item revealing that a Stuyvesant Falls couple "were awakened from their newly wedded bliss by a *charivari* arranged by their friends and neighbors." Well, my thoughts immediately turned to the derivation of the word *charivari,* which to say the least, is obscure. In France it was used to designate a wild tumult, an uproar or a din created by the beating of pans, kettles and metal dishes. This racket was combined with whistling, bawling and groans.

During the Middle Ages in France, this serenade, if it can be called such, was conducted against persons who had married twice. The widow was particularly assailed. The participants, usually masked, recited and sang satirical, indecent songs and would not let up until the terrified newlyweds shelled out some sort of ransom. If an older man took unto himself a bride of tender years, the uproar and commotion tripled in volume.

In some parts of Columbia County, this custom of serenading newlyweds prevails today. We recall a real, old-time hair-raiser that took place in Old Chatham a number of years ago. "Tonight they're planning to 'horn' Ellie and Bert. They just got back from their honeymoon at Niagara Falls."

This choice bit of news had spread throughout the community at Joe Zoch's bar, at Bernie Redmond's store and was carried into the hinterlands by the letter carrier and Ken Meier in his "Traveling Market," an ancient school bus stashed with comestibles to be purveyed to farm families. Party telephone lines were busy that day, too, and at the Rutland Railroad depot the "hornin'" was the topic of the day.

Two weeks previously, Ellie and Bert had been "spliced" in a Saturday afternoon ceremony at the stately Old Chatham Methodist Church. Then they were driven to Albany where they took the "Honeymoon Express" to "Niagary Falls."

Peepers had just joined in their evening chorus in the gathering dusk when men, women and children along with a pack of assorted dogs, gathered in front of Redmond's Store. Everyone was armed with something that would make a din—cowbells, milk pans, sleigh bells, musical instruments including several trombones and bass drums. The mother and father of the bridegroom had been alerted to the impending onslaught. Hearing the shuffling of feet and muffled talk, Pa armed himself with two big pitchers and scuttled to the cellar, turned the spigot on the hard cider barrel. The liquor that poured out was filled with sparking bubbles. It was hard with the kick of a mule.

Ma opened the back door of the house on Depot Lane. Neighbors slid quietly in with pans of fragrant beans, cole slaw, "scalped potatoes," roasted fresh hams, turkeys and capons, freshly baked breads and a bevy of multi-hued layer cakes. Gallons of black coffee began to simmer in the wash boiler. While the ladies arranged the collation, the menfolk fortified themselves with a belt of Kinderhook apple jack at Mr. Zoch's bar.

It was dark now and the crowd became restless in the village square. Whispered commands were given dogs and children to be quiet. The newlyweds had retired to their nuptial bed on the second floor of the present post office building. The light in their bedroom snapped off. Moments later, Ellie and Bert were aroused from their amorous pursuits by a cacophony of sounds that made the Battle of the Bastille pale by comparison.

Gunfire split the night air. Usually placid, God-fearing families screamed, shrieked and caterwauled. Children and dogs joined in. Drums boomed, metal rasped against metal, trombones wailed, thimbled fingers danced over washboards. The engineer on the northbound Rutland Railroad joined in the din as he hauled down on the steam whistle all the way from Powell's Crossing to the depot. The bride clutched her husband around the neck in terror.

He pulled himself loose and squinted out the window. "It's a hornin'," he whispered. "Get your clothes on, we'll have to face it." Ellie refused to budge from the room.

Many years later, she confided, "I never would have gone down, but just as I was pulling my dress over my head, I looked toward the window, and there stood Rack Bates staring at me. He'd shimmied up the porch pillar and was on the roof."

At last the newlyweds appeared and were swept up in an impromptu parade that took one turn around the huge maple tree in the square and then headed for the bridegroom's parents' abode on Depot Lane. The horners swarmed into the house for food and drink. Bob Lank, the Malden Bridge postmaster, had brought his violin—just in case. He struck up "Swing that Gal" and bellowed, "Choose your partners." The dancing started, glasses were raised time and again to the newlyweds, wishing them years of happiness and scads of children.

The tables, once loaded with an array of foodstuffs, were soon emptied and shoved to one side of the room. By midnight, three more fiddlers had appeared on the scene and the dancers followed their command to "Dive for the oyster, dig for the clam, and you'll end up in a happy land." More cider was hauled in from the cellars in Hansonville, Rider's Mills, and Seven Bridges Road. The celebration lasted until almost milking time.

Continuing her confidence, Ellie later said, "I never knew who did it, but I had my suspicions. Somebody sneaked upstairs and emptied a whole pot of baking soda into the chamber pot under the bed. It was years before I was able to live it down."

They don't do parties like that anymore and that's probably good news for those who have just entered the blissful temple of married life.

———⪢◆⪡———

No Bottom Pond . . .
Yesteryear's farmers knew death lurked beneath this sparkling
jewel in the Austerlitz Mountains

One of the most famous yet rarely visited bodies of water in Columbia County is No Bottom Pond, located in a remote, mountainous area of the Austerlitz Hills known as the Fog Hill District. Years ago, when farmers kept hundreds of sheep browsing on the nearby hillsides, the pond was a favorable picnic spot and many Austerlitz gallants accompanied by nervous young ladies would hitch up the family horse and set out for a Sunday afternoon in this mysterious and foreboding section. Aroused and fired with expectations of coming thrills and fortified with generous baskets of luncheons, the young couples would make visits to No Bottom Pond an all-day venture.

These exploration parties ascended to the district about which stories have been told and retold around the crackling fires of a winter hearthside, as now and then a pitcher of cider went the rounds. All of these tales were gospel truth according to the age and sweetness of the cider and the degree of temperature outside.

The pond has changed little in the past half century. The fields where sheep once grazed are now covered with heavy growth of alder, pines and birch with only moss-covered stone to show the outline of farm properties. It is still one of those beautiful bodies of water which appear to be fathoms deep in springtime. Dark blue and cold are the waters as they reflect the delicate pussy willows that abound. Wood duck, disturbed from a languid dip, swirl off over the sighing pines and into a cloudless sky.

By the time the glorious Fourth of July rolls around, the pond is usually as dry as salt herring. Except, of course, the deep, well-like hole amid the rocks where a good-sized stream seems to bubble out of the ground and then entirely disappears, swallowed by the earth, only to reappear again at the surface as it runs off to the east and the lands of Canaan township. It is into this abyss, rumor had it, that a man once slipped and was never seen again. Tales are still told in Red Rock of an ox that fell into this pit and disappeared forever from human sight. The farmer who owned the ox threw rocks into the hole somehow expecting they would help the doomed animal.

No doubt they did. Each boulder only gave it a push toward its ultimate destination—the land of Canaan.

Age-hollowed caverns surround the pond and have frequently been visited by "spelunkers," that species of human who enjoys a Sunday afternoon in the dank, damp recess of a Neolithic cave. Paleontologists who have visited the area are almost sure that an unusual siphon action sucks waters from deep within the earth to fill No Bottom Pond and then by some gigantic, unforeseen force, the water is drawn back into the cavernous hole which gives the pond its name.

This belief is borne out by the fact that the pond can suddenly go dry in the midst of a long, wet spell but will be up again in the middle of a summer drought. The pond was long a favorite haunt of the famous Austerlitz hunter, the late George "Pop" Sweet, who lived but a partridge flight from the great, blue pool. Wildcats abound in the woods here and "Pop," along with many other hunters, saw what they described as an "enormous black cat" which purportedly lived in a cave near the pond. This gave rise to tales of "the Black Beast of the Berkshires," a fearsome catamount which feasts on farm cattle all the way along the Taconic Mountain range into the fertile fields of Connecticut.

One of the twice-told tales of No Bottom Pond concerns a family who lived in the Austerlitz back country and "took in" boarders during the summer months. The locality was and still is perfectly adapted for such a project. The scenery is outstandingly beautiful, the air crisp and invigorating. To this boarding house there came not too many years ago a young man from the metropolitan area of New York. His name was never recorded at this farm home, but people who recall the incident remember the youth as devil-may-care with a fervent desire to explore the pond and its surrounding limestone caves.

It was in the spring of the year and his host and hostess filled him with good food, grog, and exciting tales of wild cats and bears that roamed the far reaches of the Austerlitz Hills. On a bright, clear morning the visitor, armed with a shotgun supplied by the owner of the boarding house, set out on his safari through the hills. He was never seen again. A search was conducted by men who knew the woods thoroughly but no sign was ever found of the city youth, although his gun was found near the edge of the water.

The most logical conclusion reached by Austerlitz residents that summer as they sat on the porch of the boarding house was this— the boy had fallen into the abyss at the pond, or he may have found his way into one of the caverns and wandered for miles and miles through subterranean passages, until he came at last to a different land, and there remained. Perhaps he is still living to a ripe, old age without ever sending the mistress of the boarding house as much as a postcard to acquaint her with his new surroundings. The tale has been embellished through the years as it has been quietly related on the sweet stillness of a spring night or told in louder tones to overcome the wailing of winter winds. But despite many doubtful listeners, none have been able to prove that death doesn't lurk beneath the sparkling jewel deep in the pine woods on Fog Hill.

Happy Memories of . . . Moonglow on Queechy

Dining at Queechy Lake can be a most pleasing experience. On a bright June day this week we breakfasted by an open window overlooking what has been described as "a pearl of water in the Berkshires," and my mind drifted back to the carefree days of my youth spent at the lake. Invariably, every year I fell in love with some attractive damselle from the city who summered at the lake, and every September there was a sad parting as the young lady left Columbia County for her distant home.

Winter snows usually froze romantic cogitations of the summer past but, when June returned to the calendar, it was once more off to Queechy and into the arms of Eros for another amatory pursuit. The summer of 1936 I worked at the *Chatham Courier* under the tutelage of editor Clifford Hodge, who assigned me to the sports editor's slot. How could I possibly intertwine athletics and Queechy Lake? Easy. In those days there was a particularly fine boys' camp at Queechy, appropriately named Boyville. Here, each summer, came the male offspring of well-to-do families, and the camp roster included such names as Roosevelt, Cabot, Lodge and Dupont.

In my juvenescence I imagined *Courier* readers might be extremely interested in the happenings at Boyville. With camera in hand, I went to the camp and was welcomed by the Mueller family, the owners. Each afternoon, the boys paddled long Indian canoes across the lake waters to the Berkshire Farm swimming beach, and I rode along snapping photos. I duly reported the results of volleyball, horseshoes, swimming competition and myriad other athletic events. Once I had these compiled in my notebook, it was off to the swimming float just off the Washburn property, a gathering point for Chatham's teen-age swain. Here we would ogle the visiting lovelies and perhaps invite them to join us that evening at the Queechy Lake casino, but more on that later.

Then I would hop in the Model A Ford Phaeton that I had purchased from Abrams and Boright for $38, and hustle back to the *Courier* to write my copy. The Model A, by the way, had no top, the fenders were hanging loose and it frequently boiled over, but it got me to Queechy and back and that's all that mattered. Editor Hodge came quickly to the conclusion that there were events other than the sportive endeavors of Boyville's campers that might be of interest to his readers and my almost daily visits to Queechy were promptly curtailed. Alas!

Here we are back at the Queechy Lake hotel and chatting with Frances Veillette, who, with her daughter, Jeanne, lend a gentle air of proprietorship to the inn. Over a second cup of coffee we dipped back into history and recalled the Stockbridge Indians were probably the first North Americans to enjoy the crystal-clear lake waters. The lake, first known as Whiting's Pond, was later named Queechy for a popular 19th-century novel by Susan Warner, who spent her summers in Canaan. For more than 150 years the lake has been a mecca for summer visitors. In the post-civil war period, families moved from urban centers to spend July and August at the many boarding houses found in the vicinity of Canaan. For most of these visitors there was little entertainment except for bathing or an occasional family picnic. Not until the boys returned from France after World War I did bathing and picnics cease to be the principal source of amusement for Queechy's visitors. Model T Fords brought more and more of the misnomered "Flaming Youth" of the 1920s to Queechy Lake and there they found a low, rambling building where they could release their pent-up energies.

It was in 1922 that Richard George Smart of Woodhaven, N.Y., moved to Canaan with his wife and two children, Frances and George. With the aid of Andrew Thomas, a Canaan carpenter, he built a small refreshment stand on the lake shore not far from Queechy's outlet into the Canaan brook. The Smarts were an instant success with their homemade ice cream and soon added an extension to their building which included a dance pavilion.

The refreshment stand with its new addition was now the Queechy Lake Casino, boasting "the best dance floor in New York

State." Teen-agers came by the hundreds to enjoy the music of Lee Rose and his "Radio Recording Orchestra." On Saturday nights the casino literally rocked as youngsters gyrated through the intricate steps of the Charleston. By the fall of 1927, the long porch which extended over the lake had to be shored up after a summer of pummeling by dancing feet. No liquor was ever served at the casino, and because of this parents permitted their offspring to enjoy evening after evening on the dance floor or view the new "talking pictures." George Smart had shown silent films for several years at the casino, but then signed up Harry Lamont of Valatie to bring "talkies" to Queechy Lake.

Mr. Lamont traveled the resort circuits with a screen projector and made twice weekly visits to the casino on Wednesday and Saturday nights. For the sum of 25 cents for adults and 15 for children, families enjoyed Al Jolson in *The Jazz Singer,* Wallace Beery in *Behind the Front* and watched Clara Bow portray a spicy bit of femininity in *It.*

By the 1930s, a new generation had discovered Queechy Lake and there was now a rivalry between the casino and the Canaan Community Club, which was just down the road apiece. Both were sponsoring dances and movies. The casino gradually pulled into the lead over the C.C.C., although Mr. Smart, who had guided the destinies of his dining and dancing emporium, died in 1933. Now it was Mrs. Smart and her children, George and Frances, who planned the summer activities.

In July 1934 they opened the season with Pete Vitton and his orchestra, a popular Pittsfield dance band. On alternate weekends there was square dancing to the squeaking fiddles of "Pop" Sweet and his Huckleberry Pickers. "Pop" and "Ma" Sweet had gained some national prominence following a radio interview with Lowell Thomas and by the fact they had played some Austerlitz foot-stompin' music ensconced on a platform in one of R. H. Macy's windows, in Gotham.

The halcyon days for the casino were in the late 1930s just before World War II. The big bands were at the height of their popularity and the Smarts had booked the best big band in the Berkshires—"Duke" Milne's 11-piece orchestra out of Pittsfield. The band played the best of the Miller, Dorsey, Goodman and Shaw arrangements.

Everything on the lake seemed to come to a complete stop on one of those soft, warm July nights of yesteryear when, from the casino, the slow melodic notes of "Moonglow" floated over the dark waters and drifted into the pine groves on the opposite shore. Moments later the quixotic trance would be broken when the old porch over the lake would once again take pounding from those new feet as they danced "the Shag" while "Duke" Milne led the band through "The Casa Loma Stomp."

In 1941, George Smart, Jr., entered the service and by 1942 the boys who had danced the night away the summer before were now doing close-order drill. As a result, the casino closed forever. It was eventually sold to the late Edward Jacobson, a Canaan artist who tore down the old structure and built the Berkshire Art Center, which had a brief but successful life.

Today the casino is but a memory. On quiet summer nights, however, couples now in their golden years may stop by the lake shore to hopefully hear once more a sweetly flowing arrangement of "Stardust" or "Moonglow" wafting out in the night air. Granddad, who is driving, will turn to the grandchildren in the back seat who they are taking out to dinner, and recall with a touch of nostalgia, "You know, kids, this is the very place where I met your grandmother."

To which will come the reply, "OK, Granddad, let's put it in orbit, we'll be late for McDonald's *Jurassic Park* special." Another era—another generation.

Yesterday's Hayin' Time on the Farm

Haying time is almost over on our country farms, except later, come early autumn, there will be a second growth or "aftermath" and what a monstrous crop there has been this year, thanks to those torrential rains in May. The bumblebees have been on a spree in the red clover patches, which have never seemed so red or in such abundance.

As we approach the 21st century, it's a rarity to know of a farmer who keeps a pair of horses, and a field of timothy is a rare treat. Timothy is a horse fodder named for Timothy Hanson who was the first to cultivate it in this country. The English farmers called it "meadow cat's tail" and introduced it to the American colonies in the 18th century. Before today's mammoth modern machinery, "hayin' time" was greatly different.

In anticipation of the "right time to cut," the blades for the mowing machine had to be sharpened by the local blacksmith, or more often at home on the grindstone. A rusty can, with a hole in the bottom, suspended from a rod, dripped slowly on the turning grindstone wheel. This kept the stone wet as a sweating, panting farm lad turned the handle. Fortifying himself with a fresh chaw of plug tobacco, and a jug of switchel under his arm, the hired man hitched the team to the mowing machine and drove to the hay field.

If the sun shone brightly and a good breeze was blowing, the hay would be dried by afternoon. But before driving the hay into the barn, a single horse would be hitched to the "tedder." The rear of this machine had many gadgets that resembled an enlarged grasshopper's legs, and these kicked the hay in the air and spread it for thorough drying. As early as 1557, some muse wrote, "The grasse being cutte must be well tedded."

The hay rake was first used in 1857; a two-wheeled device, it was hitched to a single horse. Riding on it for hours was far more effective than the manipulations of a chiropractor. Slipped discs had not been heard of in that era of American farming. The rake would be drawn through the hay, and the tines, tripped by a foot pedal, released the hay. The hay was raked in windrows, then the farmhands came with their pitchforks and mounded the hay into cocks.

Then into the field came the hay wagon pulled by a chunky pair of horses, switching their tails and shaking their manes to dislodge swarms of persistent horse flies.

"Keep your behind to the load," the novice was advised if he was seen trying to pitch a forkful in front of him. The horses were driven slowly as the hired man, standing on the load, skillfully placed the hay. The hay had to be laid evenly, otherwise the whole load might slide off on the way to the barn. It was a backbreaking task for farmers to pitch hay from the wagon up into the hayloft, but the ingenious Shakers thought of a better way that saved hours of labor. The great stone barn on Mount Lebanon was three stories high and the barn floor was wide enough to drive in a team of horses. The mows were *below* and the hay could be pitched down instead of up.

Today's diesel-powered behemoths that cut, chop and bale hay all in one operation have removed, forever, yesteryear's haying methods. No one drinks switchel anymore and few of today's farmers chew tobacco. On occasion on some abandoned farm, half buried in burdocks and nestles, one can still see the rusty skeleton of a horse-drawn mowing machine or hay rake.

Maude Miller "in tattered dress and bare of foot" no longer "rakes the meadow sweet with hay." Even that meadow minstrel, the bobolink, is seldom seen.

I well recall as a lad working on the Kelly farm in New Britain, and after a sizzling day in the field, hearing Johnny Kelly say, "I guess it's time for you to go after the cows." That meant a quick dip in a nearby stream and walking the cows back to the barn as the long shadows of early evening stretched over the fields redolent with the scent of new-mown hay. There was a sense of accomplishment at the end of a long July day.

⊰•⊱

Fond Memories of Long Ago Sweet Summers

June is gone and now July's vivid lightning fills the skies. The glorious Fourth is but a memory, and before we know it, the days will be a tad shorter, the crickets' evensong will be a few measures faster as August approaches, loosestrife will blanket swamplands, the Chatham Fair signs will go up and summer will suddenly disappear. Sitting with my evening cocktail, I'll reflect on all that has been left undone and what I must accomplish tomorrow before it disappears into a non-remembered day.

Summer wasn't always like this. When I was growing up on Chatham's Payn Avenue, a perfect stillness waited for us as we stepped out of the old school on Woodbridge Ave. We had no summer school, no Little League, no summer camps, no Crellin Park, no relatives to visit. The calendar was a blank. Every day the hills between Chatham and Spencertown pressed in and the light pressed down and we had nothing to do. It was as if the planet itself had come lazily to a stop so that we could all hear the dragonflies buzzing above the creek, and the beating of our own hearts.

I recall being absolutely bored. I welcomed a chance to mow the lawn even if it meant pushing the old Sears and Roebuck rotary mower for an entire morning. The rhythmic clicking of the wheels encouraged me to sing "I've Been Workin' on the Railroad," a melody that was once Chatham's theme song. Time hung heavily on our hands in a way that it never would again. September was a distant blur. Without school to tell us who we were—fifth-graders or sixth-graders, good students or goof-offs—we were free just to be ourselves, to moon around with a head full of fantastical schemes or build tree houses or briskly staff lemonade stands. There was time for everything. Minutes were as big as plums. Hours the size of watermelons. You would spend a quarter of an hour observing the dust motes in a shaft of sunlight through the open kitchen door, wondering if anyone else could see them.

You did have one brief moment of relief from boredom if you were a Boy Scout and could afford the $12 it took to attend Camp Van Buren on Knickerbocker Lake. R. Burdell Bixby of Hudson, the county's scout executive, supervised some 100 pre-teen campers during the last two weeks in July. All of us sought to qualify for merit badges, and I chose bird watching and canoeing, a well conceived combination of sex and scouting. Here's why. Across from Camp Van Buren was Camp Orinsekwa, where nubile maidens from New York City did things girls do, including nude bathing each afternoon on their isolated beach. All we could see from Camp Van Buren were tiny white figures frolicking about in the water, too far away for a good look.

My pubescent senses told me that bird watching would provide me with binoculars and canoeing with craft that would get me next to Orinsekwa.

It worked. While fellow scouters tied knots, whipped out Morse codes with signal flags or lighted fires to cook meals, I was serenely hidden, a miniature Moses in the bulrushes, getting a sensational view of the voluptuous virgins ensconced at Orinsekwa. When I submitted my birding list, I included a "Rose-breasted Highdiver" and no one questioned it. Why should they?

Other than camp, the only respite we had from summer's heat was Lampman's Dam, a swimming hole in the Indian Creek not far from Arnold's Mills. We were not driven there by doting parents. We got there on our bicycles and rode to Buckleyville, then over a dirt road to Arnold's Mills and on to Lampman's Dam. We stayed in the deep, cool water until we turned blue, then climbed out onto the glacial stones around the pool and soaked up the warming sun.

There was a sinister streak in many of the boys who went swimming in those days. A depraved and shameless trick was to sneak back into the woods where we changed clothes, grabbed a fellow's shirt and shorts (which was all we wore), dipped them in water, tied them tightly in knots and then beat the raiments on rocks and let them parch in the sun. The victim, when it came time to leave, would literally have to pull the sun-hardened knots out with his teeth while his "friends" chanted "Chaw raw beef!" So much for horrid games of our youth.

No, I don't miss those long, slow days. What I miss is the summer time, that illusion the sun is standing still and the future is keeping its distance. Maybe that's why the two most beautiful words in the language to me are "summer" and "afternoon"—because that's when nobody gets any older. On summer afternoons, kids don't have to worry about running out of adulthood. If they have enough time on their hands, they might be one of the lucky ones who carry their summertime with them into their golden years, like the friend I once knew who wanted to go to medical school though he was 40.

"When you finish you'll be almost 55," I gasped. "I'll be 55 anyway," he replied. He's on summer time.

———⟫•◦•⟪———

Back to Mother Nature

One of my favorite summer pastimes is to take evening rides over the back country roads that criss-cross Columbia County. Recently I drove with my bride down Route 66 to Buckleyville, turned left on Arnold's Mills Road, and in Arnold's Mills, drove over Slate Hill Road to Angell Hill Road, which comes out in Spencertown. A right turn on Stonewall Road to Red Rock, then right on County Route 24 to Cemetery Road, then over the hills and finally down to Frisbee Street and home.

Passing along these byways, I was awestruck with the magnificent restoration that had transpired on many of the old homes that were falling down a few years ago. But above all, I was struck by the remoteness of those farms long before the advent of the automobile or telephone. Farm families could not contact a doctor and even if they could, winter snowdrifts often made passage impossible. So what did those good people back in Macedonia Road do on a February night when grandmother had a lingering cough? Linseed was cheap, so two tablespoons of the seed were put in a crock with slices of lemon. Then a pint of boiling water and some honey were added. It was allowed to cool and then strained. A good, hot linseed poultice was a remedy for bronchitis and pleurisy, and it didn't blister as a mustard poultice was apt to do.

Pennyroyal tea was another standby and was given a family member suffering from chills or the first sign of a cold. The family cat found plenty of catnip in the garden by the tool shed, but mother knew a good strong cup of catnip tea would reduce a fever. The common dandelion brought relief to those suffering disorders of the digestive system. An infusion was made and taken three times a day. It is said the most stubborn of warts will vanish if the milky juice from the stems is applied for several days. Every farmer's wife was an excellent nurse and had an instinctive knowledge of home remedies handed down for generations for the treatment of myriad ailments.

Taking an ounce of sunflower seeds, she placed them in a pan of water and brought it to a boil. Then it was simmered until it reduced to a pint. It was then sweetened with honey and a cupful of gin was added. Bottled and corked, it was ready to be doled out for the first hack or symptoms of a chest cold. Grandpa brewed his own and kept a sizable bottle of it in his bedside commode. Now and then he was caught downing a dose and always managed to work up a quick chest-shattering cough that fooled no one.

One quiet November night, the household was awakened by a terrific blast which rattled the window panes. It seemed to come from that part of the house where Grandpa slept. Lamps were lit with trembling hands and all members of the household scurried in that direction. There he stood in front of the open window, bare-footed in his night shirt, his double-barreled shotgun ready for another blast.

"It's them durn horse thieves from over Bloody Holler Road," he bellowed. "And I think I winged one." After that, the sunflower and gin concoction was put under lock and key.

As transportation improved, Father would hitch up the Morgan mare and drive the family into town on Sunday for dinner at the Stanwix Hotel, the present 1811 Inn, or the Chatham House. While most village enterprises closed on Sunday, Chatham's three drugstores remained open. Harry Branion and Reuben Seymour dispensed elixirs from their emporiums on Main Street. At the corner of Park Row and Depot Square was Harry Alvord's Drug Store.

This pharmacy, as they are now known, was frequented by gentlemen because, in addition to medications, the Alvords did brisk traffic in cigars and cigarettes. I well recall walking with my father up to Alvord's after attending Sunday services at St. Luke's Episcopal Church on Woodbridge Avenue.

"I'll have some 'Two-fers,' Harry," my father would say in a magnanimous tone. My own experience with smoking in those days was confined to corn silk, but I had heard about the fine cigars made in Cuba, and I was certain my father's stogies has been hand-rolled by some squinty-eyed Cuban artisan. It wasn't until later in life that I learned that "Two-fers" was an abbreviation for "two for a nickel"!

To Set or Not to Sit

When I was growing up on Chatham's Payn Avenue, almost every family had a flock of chickens, which produced a continuing supply of eggs and an occasional fat hen for Sunday dinner. My father raised Salmon Faverolles, a fancy French fowl. He was a perennial winner at the Chatham Fair poultry show because Faverolles were a rare breed and always brought home the blue ribbons in the "Fancy Foreign" variety.

As a youngster I became acquainted with "sittin'" hens or ones that wanted to "set." Hens, I learned, are set in their ways. They will hover down on anything providing it is hard and round. Take a white china doorknob, for example. A broody hen we had clutched one to her wishbone and warmed it for more than three weeks!

Those were the Great Depression years and eggs were a source of income for many families. They were taken to a village store and bartered for groceries. A few individual hens were permitted to set. Many "stole" their nests in some secluded part of the yard, usually in a thicket of nettles and berry bushes. Finally thirst, boredom and hunger would drive her off her nest. With hysterical cackling she would come weaving and tottering to the hen house for a little corn, piece of oyster shell and water. Her sisters would gather around and for a few moments she would be the center of attraction. The rooster, of course, was snubbed and not allowed to hear a word of this maternal gossip.

A few reliable ladies of the flock were permitted to set in order to strengthen next year's flock with pullets. A nest was prepared, usually in a barrel laid on its side. Fresh sod, dirt side up, was placed in it to provide moisture. Clean straw or hay would be arranged in a homey and inviting manner, and finally a clutch of 13 eggs was placed in the nest. With the aid of a flashlight, mother hen would be taken from her nest by her feet, her head hanging down. This brought a rush of blood to the brain causing dizziness. In this condition she didn't know what was going on and was gently placed on the eggs. Usually, she would settle down for three weeks of martyrdom, but often as daylight came she would skitter back to the henhouse and her favorite doorknob. Now came time for discipline. With much scolding and protest she would be removed from the nest and her cherished knob. A strip of red flannel would be tied to her few remaining tail feathers. I doubt if a hen can tell the difference between red and white, but for some reason the rag had to be red.

Removed from the henhouse and blinded by sunlight, she would be placed on the ground. Suddenly, through bleary eyes, she saw the red appendage on her posterior and took off like a scalded dog across lots. Exhausted, she would pause, mouth agape and panting, but on seeing the red streamer she would take flight again. She would be gone most of the day, but by nightfall "Biddy" would come out of the weeds and head for the henhouse, a most chastened hen. The red rag had been left on a barbed wire fence or berry bush.

There was a second technique that farm families called the "Chinese Torture." Instead of drops of water dripping endlessly on some captive's head until he went crazy, the hen got the works on the other end. A shallow pan filled with cold water would be placed on the barn floor. The hen would be placed in it and then covered with a crate. Straightening up, her head would hit the top of the box causing a stiff neck. At the urge to sit down, the cold water would touch her bare stern and she would stand again. After this treatment on a boiling July day, she was ready for anything, including laying, which she would soon start again.

The feed for my father's flock was kept in a large box by an empty box stall. It had a slanting lid held up by a stick. As the supply got lower, it took some bending to fill a measure of feed. One morning, James Henderson, a kindly and elderly black man who was our major domo, was scooping a measure of oats when "Chanty," the barnyard harem boss, spotted James' spindly shanks. The rooster, measuring the distance, got a running start, jumped in the air and sunk a spur into James' calf. Leaping up, James' arm hit the stick which brought down the lid on his head with a crash as muffled oaths (and oats) flew about the barn. Two days later, "Chanty" disappeared. That Sunday, James was invited out for dinner by "Uncle Richard" and "Aunt Sarah" Benson who lived near Borden's Pond.

"What did you have for dinner?" I asked. "Chicken," he replied with a shy smile.

POSTCARDS TO
CHATHAM

The Ballad of Union Station

Took my baby down to Union Station to catch that early train, oh, yes; said I took my baby down to the station to catch that early morning train, but the station was all boarded up, the roof falling in and don't you know that pretty much fried my brain. Sing it with me now!

Got those 'I support the idea of train travel but I don't have time to do it personally' blues. I hear that ghostly harmonica in my head and I think: If that's a ghostly harmonica in my head, where were you when it was time to buy those Harlem Division and Boston and Albany tickets to keep that harmonica all peppy and maybe buy it a drum machine? I even wonder whether the idea of train travel as a romantic rite of passage is disappearing from the land as it did in the village of Chatham, Chatham Center, Niverville, Bookview, Rensselaer and Albany. *Allllll aboard!*

Yesterday's nostalgia, Lord, there ain't nothing more pathetic than yesterday's nostalgia.

The Chatham train station, or more properly, Union Station, has gone from brave—if somewhat tattered—gentility to outright smash-mouth squalor. Something like that has happened to almost every train station; the architectural history of train stations mirrors the social history of trains.

Union Station was constructed in 1887 by the Western Railroad, later the Boston and Albany, at a cost of $65,000. The structure was designed by the Boston architectural firm of Shepley, Rutan and

Coolidge. The handsomely proportioned stone structure, with its long, extending canopies for passenger shelter, originally had a lunch room and separate waiting rooms for ladies and gentlemen. These were destroyed by fire in 1884 and were never replaced.

Lou Grogan, in his history of the Harlem Division, recalls at the beginning of the century the station served the Harlem, B&A and the Hudson branch of the B&A with more than 80 trains per day originating, terminating, making station stops or passing through the village.

Penn Central closed the station in 1962, and the ticket office façade which framed the friendly face of Edward (Bunky) Pulver, the ticket agent, now graces the office at the MacHaydn Theater. The waiting benches' last known repository was in a tavern in State Line, Mass. Oh, yes, baby, yesterday's nostalgia is pathetic, but let's glance over our shoulders and see Union Station in the 1930s.

We're standing under a canopy at the front of the station and just across the way is Signal Tower 65 and a great contraption called a water column which filled thirsty locomotives before they began their ascent of the Berkshire foothills en route to Boston. It's a Sunday afternoon and in the distance you can hear the rhythmic cadence of Train 43 moving through Buckleyville on its run from New York City to Chatham.

That huge man in the conductor's uniform is Lem Austin, and look how gallantly he guides the ladies down the stairwell. Next to him are "Brownie" Lampman and Johnny Mallon. Johnny is working this Sunday but a week from today he'll be umpiring a baseball game at the fairgrounds when the New York Central squad meets Millerton.

The evening train back to New York on Sunday nights is worth a visit to the depot. The diminutive woman in the beret is famed poet Edna St. Vincent Millay of Austerlitz, and just behind her are a couple of the nation's best known artists, John Carroll and George Luks; the man in the straw hat behind them is Hugh Lofting, who just wrote that new children's book *Dr. Doolittle*. He's been spending the summer just outside Chatham on the Valatie Road. The man shaking hands all around is Congressman Lou Rockefeller of Chatham, heading back to his desk in Washington.

Oh, I tell you, just about everyone who's anything seems to go down to New York on Sunday nights. And what a trip it is. Almost before you reach Ghent, the bar car has opened and you can have a big bourbon old fashioned for 60 cents and finish reading the *New York Herald Tribune*. By the time the big J-2b engine huffs into Philmont, the dining car is open. If you're hungry, you can have a fine repast of consommé, T-bone steak, potatoes Anna, fresh green beans, a bibb lettuce salad with vinaigrette sauce, apple pie and coffee for $1.95. Ice cream on the pie is 10 cents more.

Union Station was a cathedral of transportation in its day. There was a time when big train stations didn't smell like urine. Today's amazing fact. Union Station still stands, at least. Penn Station in New York is gone. Oh, there's something called Penn Station, but it looks like a subway stop. Grand Central is there, a living metaphor for the trashing of New York; come watch the changing of the homeless as dispirited cops roust equally dispirited citizens. Union Station was at one end of the Harlem Division and Grand Central at the other end, some 128 miles away.

Union Station, to a teenaged lad in the 1930s, seemed just as busy and impressive as Grand Central. On a winter's day, dressed in our Sunday best, my mother, father and I would arrive at the station to board a train for Albany. (My father never learned how to drive and he was a bit antsy about my mother driving on snow-covered roads.) There at the station was Charlie McKern, selling the day's papers. A wizened little man with a walrus mustache, some said he had once been a professor at RPI. The station was warm inside, the great radiators hissing steam. "Bunky" Pulver and Father exchanged pleasantries as tickets were purchased—45 cents round trip. Then it was off to Albany for shopping and dinner at Keeler's, which I topped off with a sweet mélange of ice cream and coconut called a "Snowball."

Next year will mark the 30th anniversary of the station's closing. Rumors circulate that Conrail will turn it over to Chatham village, something we have all hoped for over the years. If not, the great old edifice is going to breathe its last. It will be too far gone to restore.

As I am brooding about this, I realize that trains have just about disappeared from popular mythology altogether. I guess I was brought up in residual depression nostalgia, noble hobos and Woody Guthrie and all that. And folk songs, of course, people yearning to hear that lonesome whistle blow or, alternatively, pawning their watch and chain to ride the rails back home.

And there were the Westerns at the Crandell Theatre. The popular culture was saturated with Westerns when I was growing up and Westerns were saturated with trains. The first full-length cowboy movie ever made was *The Great Train Robbery*—pretty darned significant factoid, I'd say. Trains were always, and perhaps always will be, a part of Chatham's landscape. You'd be driving down Woodbridge Avenue and, all of a sudden, the gates would come down and a switch engine would start pushing and hauling empty freight cars onto sidings. You'd sit in your automobile counting cars for what seemed forever. When was the last time a train annoyed you?

Here's what I want to know: Now that trains have all but disappeared, how do physics teachers explain the Doppler effect?

Flying—Then and Now, First Class All the Way

Suppose you were the only journalist on that sand dune in North Carolina in 1903 and you saw the *Wright Flyer* remain aloft for 12 seconds while traveling 120 feet. Perhaps you would have thought deep thoughts, but it's equally possible that you would have sidled up to Orville and said, "Well, that's a pretty trippy way of getting across the street while lying down on a motorized kite, but it's too brief to be a viable public entertainment and too slow to be an efficient means of public transportation and, by the by, did you pack any sandwiches in that bag?"

Having failed to think deep thoughts, you might have asked Orville to think them through for you. It's possible he would have said, "Someday, I envision huge metallic airplanes spanning the oceans of the world, flying 40,000 feet above the earth while providing nine channels of stereo entertainment and a choice of complimentary beverages." It's equally possible he would have said, "You fly above the water, see, and there'd be no wake to disturb the fish and you'd just drop a line . . . "

Inventions are often smarter than their inventors.

It's also possible—no, probable—that Orville would have discussed at great length the political intricacies of the bicycle repair scene in Dayton, Ohio. It's almost certain that he would have tried to persuade you to invest in the *Wright Flyer 2.0*, a really great machine that would have all the bugs worked out and could he give you a call next week sometime?

Eighty-eight years after that memorable first flight, the great, great, great, grand progeny of the *Wright Flyer* carry millions of passengers to all points on this globe. But up there in the wild blue yonder, many of today's airplanes are in trouble—because of me. It was in the paper this week. Passengers are flying first class who have no business doing so. Nearly all first-class seats are being filled these days by interlopers and pretenders. People like me. Naturally, the regular first-class passengers don't like it. "The glamour is gone," one taken-aback passenger was quoted as saying.

The trouble is "upgrades." Most airlines will let you fly first class if you pay the full coach fare, instead of a discount fare, or if you have enough frequent-flyer credits. That's what happened recently when I cashed in my frequent-flyer coupons on a trip to San Francisco and return. I walked into the front of the airplane and stayed there. Instead of being ushered down the aisle and through the curtain, a pert hostess helped me remove my coat, motioned me to a wide window seat with leg room enough for a giraffe. This was never-never land where a hot towel awaited.

In first class you get a lot of hot towels. They give you hot towels before takeoff, after meals, before movies. The flight attendants distributed them with silver tongs, handling them ever so gingerly, like rare stamps. "Care for a hot towel?" the attendant asked. She addressed me by my first name. I had never met her before, but she knew my name because this was first class. They are always giving you things in first class—a little blue notebook, a sewing kit, a pair of slippers, a toothbrush. I didn't use them, but it's the thought that counts.

We took off; the first-class section of the airplane left the ground an instant before the rear section. They think of everything. In first class, you see things out of the window a little bit before the rest of the aircraft does. If you're outside the continental limits, you enter U.S. airspace before the rest of the folks in the back do. And you get fancy headphones that don't stick in your ears like ice picks. The flight attendant doesn't hit you up for $4, either. In coach class, to see the movie, I usually had to peek around a drooling, yowling baby in the seat ahead or peer over the *Wall Street Journal* held by an elderly gentleman who capably moved the newspaper each time I twisted my head to improve my line of vision.

In first class, when you stop watching the movie halfway through because it's so stupid, you feel less of a chump.

If you are a guzzler, first class is absolute heaven. You don't have to wait while attendants struggle up and down the aisle with a beverage cart. Oh, no, not in premiero class. The moment I was seated, the attendant handed me a beverage list. It was still early morning, breakfast had not been served, but here were all these enticing libations GRATIS! I chose a Bloody Mary, which was in a chilled glass complete with a feathery celery stalk.

They served breakfast. Not in a plastic box as the peons in the rear were receiving. Crisp linen was draped over the serving tray, and on another tray was presented a fruit compote, followed by eggs Benedict, croissants, a large slice of sweet butter and a French confiture, plus cups of steaming coffee.

I felt a bit self-conscious about enjoying this meal. The newspaper story said the airplane spent $7 on my breakfast, instead of the $2.50 on the meal it was spending for the folks in steerage. The same airline said it was losing $250 million a year. Look what happens when you let enough of us frequent flyers into the front of the airplane.

But a curious phenomenon was occurring and, fortunately, I didn't notice it. The entire first-class section on this flight was full. Coach class was half empty. I asked the flight attendant if it was appropriate and possible to downgrade my upgrade. She said yea, it was (again calling me by name), parted and called out a soft "Goodbye" as I slipped back among the people. I found one of those five-across benches with no one on it. I flipped up all the arm rests and lay down. It was a lot more comfortable than first class. And when we touched down at JFK, with rear wheels first, the folks in steerage were actually home an instant before the first-class riders up front. It didn't even cost extra.

——————◆◆◆——————

Driving in Mexico

SAN MIGUEL DE ALLENDE—It's a long way to Tipperary, the old song reminds us, but it's even a longer way from Chatham to this hillside mountain town in Central Mexico—3,740 miles, to be exact. Driving on interstate highways in the U.S. becomes boring, but the moment you cross the international border and enter Mexico, defensive driving becomes a matter of life or death. We crossed the border at Laredo, Texas, and entered Nuevo Laredo, Mexico. We were immediately surrounded by normally mild-mannered inoffensive Mexicans who, once they get behind the wheel of an automobile, become kamikazes.

Here, in San Miguel, I was introduced to the Jekyll-Hyde Mexican driver about a decade ago when I hailed a taxi. The man behind the wheel was pleasant and smiling when I gave him the address, but almost immediately he turned into a snarling, vicious maniac. Every car and every person was his enemy, unable to do anything right. With his mutterings and dark forebodings about their ancestry, especially the type of woman their mother no doubt was, he found no good in mankind.

He jerked his cab by the front and back bumpers in and out of traffic, just daring anyone to give him a fair shot at them even for a microsecond, and he certainly intended them to end up in perdition. At last, when he stopped by the curb to let me out, he again had an almost benign, saintly smile on his face. Needless to say, I drew a deep satisfying breath of air as I dismounted, because I had not dared to breathe or look to the right or left during the entire ride.

My second, related incident involved not so much the Jekyll-Hyde driver, but a Mexican friend of mine who, when he drives, is interested in everything except the driving. He observes everything on both sides of the road as well as what is in front of him and behind him. Juan Carlos is an agricultural agent here in the state of Guanajuato, and a very good agent. He loves to observe crops, trees, animals, deserts, forests and just anything that nature provides, and nature generally provides plenty in Mexico. The only problem is that he is not interested in where the pavement starts or ends, on either side of the road. Highway dividing lines are just a waste of good paint as far as Juan Carlos is concerned. He wanders from side to side at 65 mph, never slowing down for dangerous curves, but he never misses seeing any of the wildlife—deer, coyotes, turkeys, armadillos—along the way.

Well, the fatalistic part was, have a heart attack or relax. So I relaxed with this thought in mind: if we hit something, we'll all be killed. Calmed by that, I happily laid my head abroad and took a nap with one eye open.

On a recent trip from San Miguel with friends of ours, we took their car and so it meant the other man drove. He was new to driving in Mexico and he, too, had that real killer nature. The curves were not meant to be an object to get around, but something to attack. Other cars and trucks were enemies and had no business being on the road. If the car had brakes, I never could discern it. Brakes were surplus equipment. The car did not have handles inside that were attached to the roof when we hit a "tope."

On the outskirts of every Mexican community, drivers will find "topes," small barriers to slow down traffic. In the States we call them "thank you ma'ams." Now, an eight-inch-high tope can certainly do something to the car, the driver, and passengers when it's hit at 50 mph. I would have gladly cried "Geronimo!" at that first tope but the breath was knocked out of me and I was scrambling to find the missing seat under me. My bottom and the seat did reunite, but they will never be the same again.

Now the moral of my story: Mexico's roads and Mexican drivers are not the same as in the States. Just as you do when driving in England, France or Germany, you must make adjustments for local habits and conditions. Most roads in Mexico are narrow. The shoulders drop off precipitously in many areas. There is no room for error. A slow or medium speed allows you adjustment time; fast does not. The faster you drive, the more danger you invite. On curves and hills you certainly don't know what you will find on the other side. There could be a car, truck or bus parked. The road could be under repair with no signs or barricades posted. A horse, burro or cow could be looking into your windshield. Don't chance it!

When meeting traffic, if the oncoming car has its lights on, you had better give ground quickly. The lights mean the driver can't get back into his lane and wants the right-of-way.

Do not drive at night unless there is no other way. Vehicles or wagons may be parked on the road with no lights. Animals can be an extreme hazard during hours of darkness.

Also, when driving in Mexico and your gauge is on the half-full mark, stop at the next Pemex station. The green pump is marked "Magna Sin," the best of Mexico's unleaded gas. Check the pump first to make sure that only zeroes show. Some sly Mexicans leave a few thousand pesos on the pump in the hopes that you won't notice them.

Should you become involved in a wreck—this is not the U.S. Whether you have insurance and whether you were at fault, unless you want to spend several days in jail, the driver should leave the car sitting and get the hell out of there. Go to a lawyer and let the attorney handle the situation. If fortunate, you may be 95 percent in the right; if unfortunate, you'll be 100 percent in jail unless you "vamoose."

Mexican driving can be fun and interesting, The best plan is not to push it and not take your life in your hands for the sake of a few extra minutes. Remember, this is *mañana* land—you want to be around *mañana* to enjoy it. *Hasta la vista!*

Making Life a Success

SAN MIGUEL DE ALLENDE—A Mexican physician invited us for dinner. We showed up an hour late and nobody noticed. We didn't sit down at table 'til midnight. A mariachi band was playing as though it were noon.

"Mexicans don't care about time," the doctor said. "We are more concerned with affection and sensation. People here are very emotional. If I run a stop sign and a policeman catches me, I can make an explanation. If I am convincing, he might let me go. Not so in the United States of America."

Dr. Federico Zavala went to medical school at Cornell. Had a practice in New York for a time. He has made a study of the differences between the Mexican and the U.S. way of thinking.

"Americans are tied to work. I think they're lonely people because of it," he said. "We have a more free society here. You want to be more efficient. We want to be joyful. You want to make a successful life. We want to make life a success. There's a difference."

He said he couldn't understand why Mexicans are rapped for their joyful inefficiency.

"We're very much like the Irish," he said, "and the Irish are beloved for their behavior. Why is that?"

Zavala visits the United States often. He has difficulty deciding which society is better.

"It's harder to succeed in Mexico," he said. "If you follow the rules in the U.S. you are likely to succeed. In Mexico, there are no fixed rules. You are on your own."

Mexican money continues to fall against the dollar at the rate of about two pesos a week. At this writing, the exchange rate is 2958 pesos for one dollar. When I first visited Mexico in 1962, the rate was eight pesos to a dollar. Students find it nearly impossible to pay for textbooks printed in the United States. Opportunities to study abroad have been pretty well shut down.

Dr. Zavala said: "If you see inflation and our great national debt as an American, you see a real problem. A Mexican takes the view that it will all pass. The Mexican government should not try to fashion our economy after the U.S. industrial model. We are an agricultural country. The United States of Mexico cannot be the United States of America."

There is no unemployment insurance in Mexico. But employers must give three months' salary plus vacation pay to workers they lay off. It's cheaper to keep people on the payroll. That's why restaurants have more help than they need. There are plenty of waiters and bus boys. Always someone to light your cigarette. But they tell you they hate to bring you your check.

The doctor said: "They do not wish to halt the festive event that is your dinner. The check says that it's time to go. They don't want to tell you that. They want you to enjoy yourself. There is no rush."

He said: "If you live here, you must forget about the pace of life in the USA. *Mañana* is an important concept. If you are exasperated by the Mexican pace and show it—you are in big trouble. Which society is better?" the doctor asks and replies. "Hard to say. But mostly Americans who come to Mexico want to stay here. And more Mexicans who go to the USA hope to return."

On your first visit to Mexico you will perhaps for the first time experience what seasoned travelers call "cultural shock." My definition of cultural shock is the sudden realization that people are different. They speak a different language, they have a different set of values, they see the world a little differently than you do. It's hard to put your finger on it, but you know something is different. Cultural shock can be a pleasant experience. It can also ruin your vacation. Courtesy, plain common courtesy (as well as common sense) can do much to ease this realization of cultural differences.

Patience is a virtue in Mexico. Nobody seems to be in a hurry. Things happen, but they happen at a slower pace. Nothing seems to be immediate and there is a lack of any sense of urgency. This is especially true in the tropics and it is one of the many tropical lures.

In Mexico, patience must be extended to verbal communications. You may speak no Spanish or remember a little from your high school course years ago. A Mexican who serves you in a restaurant or in a store may speak just a smattering of English. Through patience, communication is possible. Words are not the only way to communicate. A happy face, a smile, a laugh can bring about communication. But an effort must be made. Impatience, the loss of temper, getting upset, loud words will accomplish nothing. Patience will be one of the ingredients that will insure a good time on your vacation. It goes a long way.

The worst thing one can do on vacations is to make comparisons. If we really want things "just like home"—why did we leave home in the first place? Making comparisons can only frustrate the reality right at this moment. The present is never given a chance and the moment is gone forever. If ever the urge to make comparisons overcomes me, I direct dial a friend in Kinderhook, East Chatham, or Philmont on a winter night.

"How's the weather?" I ask.

There follows a summary beginning "brutal cold, chilling winds and more snow tomorrow." I compare that forecast with the Mexican night I am enjoying. Sparkling stars in a black sky, the fragrance of oleander, jasmine and orange blossoms mingling on soft, cool zephyrs wafting up the mountainside, the stillness of the evening and the promise of an absolutely perfect day on the morrow. In those comparisons, I rejoice.

Washing Made Easy—Down Mexico Way

SAN MIGUEL DE ALLENDE—Shortly after our arrival here, our housekeeper, Eva, announced that our washing machine had reached the end of the line; the loud clanking that it produced indicated as much. Feeling in an expansive (and expensive) mood, I volunteered to contact Sears Roebuck in the nearby city of Queretero, where a well-meaning friend had assured me, Sears carries a splendid line of washing machines. Not knowing Sears' number and wanting to know if they would be open Saturday afternoon, I dialed "information."

"Could you give me the number of Sears Roebuck in Queretero?" I asked.

There was a moment of silence and then "Un momento."

The "momento" turned into a very long "momento," at which point the operator said, "There is no such name."

"WHAT! The Sears is one of the biggest stores on earth; the branch in Queretero is just a half block off the plaza."

"Oh," she screamed, "you mean SAHRS!"

Fully chastened by my mispronunciation, I found that SAHRS would definitely be open until 8 P.M. on Saturday, so I drove over to Queretero. Indeed, there was a splendid line of washing machines, dozens of them all glistening white and marked "IMPORTADO." The array of knobs, buttons, tunes, dials, arrows and something that looked like a multicolored clock clearly rivaled the control board of a jet aircraft.

Realizing my inability to select from such a display, I put myself in the hands of an overly cordial salesman who spoke English. He promptly urged me to acquire something called a "Hotpoint," which carried an astronomically high price tag but had been marked down. It was the very best of the line, he assured me, simplicity itself to operate and it was guaranteed to last practically forever. I pulled out the plastic and became its owner.

Three weeks and four phone calls later, at 8:30 P.M. one night, two tired-looking men and a truck appeared at our home with the washing machine. They hastily unloaded it and barely gave me time to sign the receipt book, which indicated they had been covering most of central Mexico in the last 75 hours delivering other washers; ours being the last.

It was much too late to admire our acquisition, but the next morning Eva, our housekeeper and I assembled in the patio where her husband, Jesus, had erected something reminiscent of a Diego Rivera Monument to the Revolution on which the washer was now standing. It had a semicircular raised base, four posts, a corrugated asbestos roof and was set against a wall topped by Eva's many-flow-ered pots.

The ensemble was a work of art, as evidenced by the fact that one of Jesus' sons had dropped by a few days earlier and had asked his father if he was getting ready for "Day of the Altars"—an annual Easter-season event when Mexican families decorate the windows and doorways of their homes with flower-filled altars.

The knobs, dials, clock, etc., were still much in evidence as we opened the washer lid and extracted a most impressive document, the size of a small dictionary. It was entirely in ENGLISH.

"No problem," I assured Eva and Jesus, "I will translate."

"Starting on the far left (west side), it says, 'silk'; that means 'seda.'"

"But you don't have anything made of silk," said the house-keeper.

Ignoring this truth, I continued eastward along the gadgets: "Here it says 'cotton,' that means 'algodon.'"

"Everything is made of acrylic now," commented Eva.

My eye finally fell on something that surely would draw a most enthusiastic response; the dial was marked "Permanent Press."

"This means 'planchada permanente,'" I explained.

"You did have two pairs of pants with that tag," said Eva, "but the press disappeared and I use a hot iron on them now."

Still undaunted, I evolved farther eastward and was amazed to read "light soil" and "normal soil." This sounded like something the Columbia County Cooperative Extension office would employ in a spring gardening article. Stranger still was another sign that said, "handwash"; if true, why had I bought an automatic washer?

One thing especially worried me, the word "WARNING" on the instructions which advised that without the utmost care in ground-ing the apparatus, there would be definite likelihood of electrocution.

I had visions of Eva stretched out stiffer than a stake, but when I described this danger in dramatic terms, both she and Jesus considered it extremely funny. Mexican fatalism, no doubt.

Jesus was now making a careful examination of the more fundamental installation problems of the washer; he even asked me what "hot water" meant. I explained "hot water" in some detail only to have the housekeeper remark that there wasn't a hot water connection within miles of the patio and she expected to use a pail on the rare occasions when she didn't wash in cold water.

By now, if it had been the hour for a stiff drink, I would have them make one, but it seemed best to retire discreetly and see what Jesus and Eva would do alone. Some time later, I asked Jesus how they were progressing. "Oh, it's all put together and ready to go," he said. "No hay problema."

Feeling that a modest celebration was in order, but lacking a brass band and holy water, we all gathered about the machine as Jesus proudly threw the switch. It hummed and gurgled a moment then stopped. We tried pushing every button on the appliance and setting the multi-colored clock. Nothing worked. A call to Guillermo, who is in the washing-machine repair business, brought him to the scene. One look told the story. The pipe leading to the washer was too small; a one-inch pipe solved the problem instantly.

Then, as if talking to pre-kinder infants, Guillermo explained all about washing machine "programs," which only convinced me I had mistakenly bought a computer.

Today, all is well. If any of our neighbors have a nice piece of silk they would like to wash, please drop it off at 42 Pila Seca. I'm dying to try the knob on the left.

How Warm the Sun!

SAN MIGUEL DE ALLENDE—Given the vagaries and sudden changes of climate in this mountainside community of central Mexico, and given the fact that this column must be prepared a full 10 days before publication, only a fool would try to write about the weather as it might be in two weeks from today. Hello there! Even if it means playing the fool and you dear readers back in the northland must believe me, I cannot resist the temptation today to rejoice. The Sun Is So Wonderfully Warm.

We've had weeks now of pleasantly cool, sunshiny days, days that smile faintly and ineffectually not unlike April days in Columbia County. No fun in that kind of sun, nothing that brings even a smidgen of joy to life. Now, though, we can celebrate. The Sun Is So Wonderfully Warm. It's a dilemma for some. People who get up very early (and I am sometimes included) still find a nip in the air. It's sweater weather, so they pull on a sweater as protection against the morning chill. By mid-day, though, people of both sexes are walking our street with those sweaters hanging from the waists and it's swing and sway with Tina or Jose—because The Sun Is So Warm. It's an adventure, for others, and a gamble. They dress in the morning as if it were afternoon and hasten out into the day's early briskness.

Shirtsleeves, rather then jackets or sweaters, to perhaps even the undershirts that young Mexican men sometimes wear as outershirts, are morning attire. In more ways than one, their dress code makes sense. The Sun Is Warm. More people these days are walking on the sunny side of the street. And there is more bounce in their walk, more up-and-at-'em, more sheer joy, because The Sun Is Delightfully Warm.

Cars are always parked on the street where we live. Single-parked, double-parked; the street is always full of parked cars. Too often, it's a dismal and dingy-looking sight. But not these days. These sunny days, the guy in the street who parks and washes the cars takes more pride in his work. He takes more pride because the shining sun shows off his work. He takes more pride because the shining sun shows it off to best advantage.

The cleaned chrome beams brightly, hubcaps reflect a fish-eye view of the world around them, highlights flash from the freshly washed bodies. The whole street gleams. An inspired effort all those clean cars, and the car washer was inspired because The Sun Is Warm.

Step from the shadow of a building and into the open sunlight, feel the beams pulsating into the back of your neck and tell me you don't feel a certain frostiness fleeing from your entire body. Of course you do, because The Sun Is Warm.

Back home, at another time of year, you could stand in the silent center of a farmer's field and actually hear the corn grow. Here in Mexico, these days, I can stand in my tiny garden and watch the plants' leaves seem to perk up and take notice—and all because The Sun Is Warm.

I suddenly see more red faces around town—not the red faces of embarrassment or booze, but of sunburn. You didn't know you could get a sunburn in this village? Well, you can! Especially if The Sun Is Warm.

Our house was built 150 years ago, when construction was solid, and it shows during the year's first warm and sunny days. It may be warm and sunny outside, but it's still cool inside. We may take sweaters off to go into the street, but we put them back on when we come back inside.

I join Bob and Nancy Pollard, who are visiting here from New Concord, for a sip of tequila on the balcony before lunch, my face turned up to the warming sun. I literally can feel my face turning red. The Sun Is Warm—and so is the tequila. The Pollards agree. New Concord was never like this.

Although many of you may think it strange table fare, the Cochineal cactus leaves ("Nopales") and the delicious "Indian Figs" or "Prickly Pears" ("Tunas") of the Nopal cactus are becoming favorite foods of North Americans here in Mexico. In the *mercado* (market) women busily remove the spines from the green cactus with razor-sharp knives. The cactus is sliced into julienne strips and sautéed in butter and garlic, or marinated in sugar and wine vinegar, and served like "dilly beans."

Just a while ago, in 1985, the cultivation, production and sales abroad of "nopales" and "tunas" neared semi-disaster. By 1989, exports to New York, Chicago, Los Angeles and San Diego reached 3,000 tons. And this year, 10 thousand tons will be exported to the USA, an increase of 233 percent over 1989. If you happen upon Mexican cactus all trimmed and cleaned, try it . . . you'll like it.

Mexicans believe that the cactus must be opened and penetrated before the sweet juices of its inner life, buried deep inside a prickly and foreboding exterior, will flow forth. The *fiesta* by the same token, serves to "open out" the Mexican so that his deep, hidden emotions can be expressed. In Mexico one can always find many occasions to celebrate with a *fiesta*. A Spanish student complained in a letter to the editor that her classes were always being dismissed to a restaurant because it was always someone's *cumpleanos* (saint's day). Then, of course, family events such as a *boda* (wedding) or *bautismo* (christening), especially of the first-born male heir, call for fiestas. Many families have been known to go into debt in order to outdo their neighbor with a larger and louder shindig. A party must have *ambiente* (atmosphere) and *lujo* (luxury) in addition to expected food, drink and music. If everyone has a wonderful time it is deemed a *pachanga* which could be a shortened version of *para changas* for monkeys—which would make it a rough equivalent of "as much fun as a barrel of monkeys," which most fiestas are.

⊰⟡⊱

The Story of a Little Boy and His Bird

SAN MIGUEL DE ALLENDE—Everyday life in this Mexican community is uncomplex and, from time to time, there occurs what I have described in this column as a "small-town vignette." For example, the bell of our front gate rang quite early yesterday morning. I opened it to find a small boy of seven or eight asking to come in. He pointed to the top of the great pepper tree that stands in our courtyard close to the wall. On the top branch, among entwined pink bougainvillea blossoms, sat a little green parakeet. It had flown out of its cage some distance away and was seen by a passerby who alerted the boy, the bird's owner.

I opened the gate of course, and we went together to the tree. "How are you going to get him down," I asked. "Climb the tree?" I immediately had reservations after I said this, as I did not want this little fellow shimmying up to a point 30 feet above the ground.

"Oh, no, Señor."

I offered the services of our gardener, Victorio, to get a ladder to help retrieve the bird. I didn't have a butterfly net. The boy refused all help and just said, "I'll get my bird."

So I left him standing under the tree and went into the house, poured a cup of tea, and sat by the kitchen window to see what would happen. I asked everyone not to go near the tree.

The March sun shone brightly on the terrace and I could hear the boy making soft little calls, whistles and sounds. I had our maid, Alicia, walk very quietly out with milk and cookies, all gratefully received.

The vigil continued, hours passed and sure enough, during the morning the parakeet had hopped down branch by branch. Finally, it reached a lower branch and the youngster gently grasped the bird, put in under his jacket, thanked us for the cookies and milk. I opened the gate and the boy and his bird were gone down the street. Such patience, such love. I marveled.

Our home on Pila Seca (dry well) Street leads into a section of San Miguel known as the parish of San Antonio. San Antonio is one of the poorest parishes—too poor to even have its own priest. This lovely old church, with its missing tower and crumbling wall, stands on a small incline, sadly surveying a dusty plaza with a tree or two, rocks and potholes—nothing more. Now, in the dry season, the winds blow great billows of dust which cover surrounding homes, leaving a veil of gray over all. Alicia, our maid whom I mentioned before, has a lovely voice and fills the house with music as she performs her daily tasks. She is also the chief source of music in the church on Sunday and at afternoon vespers.

When Christmas season rolls around, the parish of San Antonio stages a traditional *posada,* a reenactment of Mary and Joseph seeking a place where the Christ Child might be born.

A burro was brought out and a young girl portraying Mary was perched on top. A boy, personifying Joseph, was found to lead the burrow. Alicia led the procession singing tunes of the old and beautiful *posada* ritual as they went from house to house. As Christmas Day approached, a visiting priest announced he wished to have the church decorated.

"But, Padre, we have no money, we have no flowers . . ." It being the dry season, gardens were dormant and bare.

"Very well, then, bring your bird cages," he said.

Every Mexican home has a bird cage—indeed some two or three—and so they brought them. But first they were decorated with bits of ribbon, colored paper, lace and some even had a few flowers. They were works of art. At that time of year, flowers are scarce, but people found them. We gave Alicia permission to take whatever was blossoming in our winter garden—daisies, poinsettias, calendulas, whatever.

Alicia not only had prepared the cages of her two canaries, but borrowed ours, a fabulous singer, that she had dubbed "Pavarotti." The cages were hung and placed along the sides of the ancient church's nave. Every day they were cleaned and cared for. We were invited to attend the mass, and arrived early. The church service started. No organ music, no guitars, just Alicia and the voices of the congregation. Almost on cue, a brilliant shaft of sunlight shone down on the altar. The voices of the churchgoers rose in praise. As they sang, so sang the birds, first one, then two, then all. I doubt that the magnificent choirs of St. Peter's in Rome, of St. Paul's in London or of Washington's Cathedral were ever lovelier than the singing of the birds and the faithful in this ancient parish church.

—⊰◆⊱—

The Plight of Destitute Juan Carlos

SAN MIGUEL DE ALLENDE—The Mexican *campesinos*, the peasant farmers, have to be the hardest working people on the planet. Usually, they own a small plot of land on which they raise corn and beans to provide sustenance for their large families. Their homes are frequently no more than four walls of boards, covered with a tin roof. They have no running water, no electricity, and bathroom facilities are found only in the desert that surrounds their abode.

The story is told of Juan Carlos, an extremely poor tiller of the soil for whom everything had gone wrong. A rare frost had killed his corn and beans, his family was hungry, his children had no shoes and his wife was once again pregnant. He walked to the parish church, a distance of several miles, to offer prayers to the Almighty for relief of the suffering that he and his family had experienced. But things only got worse.

His burro, which he used to pull a wooden plow through rock-strewn fields, had bowed a tendon, and lack of rain had all but dried up the family's source of water in a nearby stream.

That night, as he gazed through a hole in the roof, a full moon shone down on his family sleeping on straw sticks spread out on a dirt floor. He arose, went outside and gazed at the sky, imploring the Lord to help. Yet, the succor he sought failed to materialize. Then Juan Carlos had another idea. He would communicate directly with the Savior by writing a letter outlining in detail his problems.

It took him the better part of a day, grasping a pencil stub in his gnarled hand, to outline his plight. He placed the supplication in an envelope and addressed it simply, "*A Dios*"—to God.

Juan Carlos then walked nine miles to the nearest village post office. Stamps were not required, he believed, to communicate directly with El Señor. He dropped his letter in a box for outgoing mail and trudged home.

A postal clerk had seen the small, gaunt figure post the letter addressed simply "*A Dios*"—and without stamps. He dutifully showed it to the postmaster who opened it and read the pitiful pleading: "Dear Lord. If you could just provide me with 100 pesos so I could buy seeds to replant my land, I shall be forever grateful.

My family and I are very hungry and we will work night and day to earn the money to repay you. I shall bring it, little by little, to church each Sunday. Thank you dear Lord, Juan Carlos"

The postmaster was touched by the farmer's simple request and passed the hat among his employees to raise the funds sought by the humble man. The peso, at the time of this story, was worth a great deal more than under this present station in the monetary world and the best the postal workers could come up with was 70 pesos.

A week later, Juan Carlos arose early and walked back to the post office where, recognized by the postal staff, he was handed an envelope with 70 pesos. Juan Carlos asked the postmaster if he might borrow a pencil, a sheet of paper and an envelope. They were immediately provided.

Going to a small table in the corner, he sat down and wrote:

Dear God,

I am so grateful you have provided me with the 100 pesos I sought of you but the BANDITS in this post office have opened your letter and taken some of the money!

Now if you could send me 30 more pesos, I shall be your faithful servant the rest of my life.

Juan Carlos

———⟫◆⟪———

Customs and Superstitions

SAN MIGUEL DE ALLENDE—In one of my recent columns, I described a visit from a witch doctor to heal an aching shoulder. The shoulder, I am happy to report, is still without pain and for that I am indebted to the *curandera* whose melodic incantations

and applications of strange lotions seemingly healed the sore afflic-
tion. The *curandera*'s charge was nominal, about $3, but some very
large fees are levied for *Limpias,* or cleansings. These are performed
to remove curses placed on you by someone else's witch doctor or
to change your luck from bad to good.

Street vendors sell amulets of myriad things from male garlic to
powdered deer antlers. There are small boxes of powders that pur-
port to stimulate the sexual libido of elderly males, while others, if
taken by a pregnant woman, will determine the sex of the child. Religious pictures with special prayers also form part of the rituals for
good health, luck, love or protection from the evil eye. These are
often long-held beliefs, going back to the days when the Aztecs and
Mayans ruled this land, and it is folly to scoff them. Merely listen—
as if they're gospel.

Mexico adheres to centuries-old customs, and violating some of
them can be taken as a personal insult or lead to your arrest. Shorts,
bathing suits, halters and miniskirts get by in the larger cities and at
the beach, but here in the provinces they are frowned upon and
scantily attired persons will probably be told by police to put some
clothes on. Ignore them and they will arrest you. They are very serious about proper dress, and up until a few years ago, women wearing long dress pants were frowned upon.

Going barefoot is a sign of poverty; it's not understood by most
Mexicans, and it is not a good idea in any event, in view that scor-
pions and black widow spiders abound in this area. Nude public
swimming is a taboo and could get you deported. When entering a
store, restaurant, home or almost any other place, you are expected
to follow the Mexican custom and greet everyone. *Buenos dias* will
do, and you reply in kind to the next person that enters. Politeness
again. At the beginning of a meal it is customary to touch glasses
and extend a *Buen provecho,* as in bon appetit, to all at the table.

Handshakes are very important. You shake hands with everyone. Knuckle crushing is unacceptable, even among the most macho men. The grasp of hands, even among men, is usually very gentle. Young children will kiss the hands of their godmothers or godfathers as well as the parish priest. The *abrazo* is a form of greeting similar to a hug. It can range from a polite touching of the upper body to a back-slapping, bone-crushing bear hug. Don't be surprised to find yourself dangling in midair and crushed to a pulp by an enthusiastic Mexican (male) friend. If you are able, by all means retaliate.

As a rule, Mexicans agree to everything but comply with what suits them best. Our practice of being straightforward and downright blunt is considered rude in Mexico. So when a Mexican agrees to meet you at a certain time, he will almost invariably be late. Time is of little import here. There's always *mañana*.

I have noticed that *soufflés* are seldom if ever served here. Why? Because if guests are invited at seven, they usually show up at eight, by which time the *soufflé* will be flat as a tortilla. Dinner is usually served about 9:30 to give errant guests plenty of time to arrive.

To save yourself embarrassment, don't admire someone else's possessions. More often than not, the Mexican will make a present of them to you. This puts you in a spot, as you will not be able to refuse the offering without seriously hurting his or her feelings, even insulting them.

Women travelers should remain aloof and inconspicuous as a defense against unwanted male attention. You should observe how the "Mexicanas" deal with men and their *machismo*. Mexican women seldom leave the house alone and travel long distances alone only when they can't find a friend, relative or neighbor to accompany them. Girl-watching is a favorite pastime among young Mexican men, who gather on street corners and in loud voices commend or condemn the feminine attributes of young women who pass by.

It is a Mexican custom to have fireworks for every public and private celebration. They usually start before sunup to announce the beginning of a *fiesta* and about 10 P.M. there will be more pyrotechnics to mark the end of the *fiesta* day. Fireworks are also used to herald the birth of a child. Boys usually rate more than girls, and twin boys are good for an earthshaking crescendo of aerial bombs just as the sun touches the mountain peaks in the east. On *fiesta* days, there are usually public announcements of fireworks displays. Join in and have a good time, but leave your wallet and camera at home.

Stay back from the towering cascades of fireworks, *castillos*, as they do throw off hot sparks. Displays in remote areas can include Roman candle battles with one crowd firing at another or rockets called *busca pieds* skittering along the ground literally "looking for feet."

There is a new mail service here that takes letters directly to Laredo, Texas, for mailing in the U.S. This cuts delivery time by a week over the mysterious Mexican postal system. But I just glanced at the clock, 2 P.M. It's *siesta* time until 4 P.M. and everything including the new direct mail service will be closed. Oh, well, there's always *mañana*.

———✦———

Do You Know What It Means to Miss New Orleans?

Color me punchy: I like to travel, but it's sort of crazy to get to New Orleans via San Francisco; but that's just what I did before we bade a farewell to old 1990. My credit card and I are worn out and I may need a new travel agent. New Orleans, the town that calls itself "The Big Easy." Congrats to the *Times-Picauyune* for a terrific headline, "Saints Win Big, Easy." Don't ask me why anybody would name a newspaper the Picayune, a word that means "trivial" or "small." As a noun, however, it once meant a small coin.

There is a never-ending battle of the cities. New Orleans vs. San Francisco. Which is the better town? This is not a multiple-choice question, which is why such answers as Paris and New York are disallowed. Size for weight, I used to think ol' Baghdad-by-the-Bay was in a class by itself, but now I'm not sure. "The Crescent City" or "The City That Care Forgot" may have only 550,000 residents, 1,300 restaurants, 650 bars and a major recession, but it puts on an impressive show. S.F. has Fisherman's Wharf. N.O. has the French Quarter—no contest there. San Franciscans keep talking about their trolley system. New Orleans has had trolleys for more than 150 years and they're still running on St. Charles Street. Ess-Eff rolls up its sidewalks by midnight, but Naw'leans has places that stay open all night, lots of 'em.

New Orleans has a longer history than S.F., but S.F. has better weather and I speak as one who has been in Bayou country in the summer. Despite the gloomy business climate, there are few beggars on the streets of New Orleans. As you would expect, the people are friendly, but people are always friendly in tourist towns. They don't say, "Have a nice day" down there; they always say, "Have a good time."

The music is terrific. Little kids walk around carrying instruments. I heard a boy about 10 playing a wah-wah trumpet in the style of Rex Steward. Yeah, Pete Fountain still plays his clarinet, but he has always been ersatz. We caught the Dirty Dozen Brass Band featuring two trumpeters blowing their brains out and three saxes doing likewise. That's music!

The amazing thing about the French Quarter is that it's commercial without being obnoxious. The commission in charge of the area must be tough because there are only a few T-shirt shops and lots of antique shops and fine art galleries, particularly the Schon Gallery on Royal Street, not to mention the seemingly endless blocks of restaurants and bars. San Francisco and New Orleans are both battling for the tourist buck and for the delegates who like to carouse at night. "The Big Easy" has it all after sundown. The term "pub crawl" must have been invented in the French Quarter.

The Garden District . . . well, the old Southern mansions with their lawns and Spanish moss and the palpable ghosts are impressive and depressing all at the same time. The district can't compare in elegance with San Francisco's Pacific and Presidio Heights, not to mention Nob Hill. Culturally, San Francisco has the edge, too. Both cities have one thing in common. They are damned dangerous.

The nice thing about New Orleans is that the locals go to the so-called tourist traps—Antoine's, Galatoire's (no plastic, cash only, no reservations), "the Quarter"—and enjoy them as much as the visitors. This makes the visitor feel good. New Orleans has only a river, even if it's a great river, where San Francisco has a bay, but the New Orleans waterfront has the most action. It's a major port. The Big Easy's new "Aquarium of the Americas" is sensational. And we spent a whole day perusing the shops in the Jax Brewery, the Riverwalk Complex and the old French Quarter, amazingly few of them of the schlocky variety.

I thought I could eat anything the New Orleans chefs could throw at me—from mumbo-jumbo-gumbo to praline cheesecake—but they found my weak spot. Garlic. I had no idea they put garlic in everything, including the ice water. The garlic bread is served entirely without bread. At the Pelican Club I was sacked for keeps by a barbonara, New Orleans style, garlic laced with pasta, oysters, clams, scallions, onions and garlic. I was out of Gaviscon and Mylanta, and in New Orleans, they laugh at Rolaids. Rolaids is for kids who had too many garlic Popsicles. I dialed 911 and got a burp.

The town is gradually getting set up for Mardi Gras, which comes early this year. Boozing is picking up but the beanies aren't exactly jammed. The manager of Galatoire's put it in familiar words: "Our regulars stay away during Mardi Gras because they think the place is full of tourists and the tourists are staying away because they think they can't get in."

Rising like a giant mushroom near Interstate 10 is the Superdome where sports freaks or convention-goers can dine on everything from Chinese to Cajun to hot dogs to daiquiris (very big here). And Hurricanes. I can imagine getting my fill of oysters, shrimp, gumbo, jambalaya and crawdads, not to mention filigreed balconies and old-time jazz. But New Orleans deserves a salute, and I bow in admiration, all the while keeping one hand on my wallet.

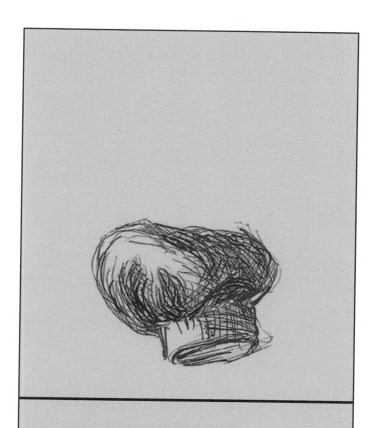

AT THE TABLE

Fondue: A Recipe for Loneliness

I hold a warm spot in my heart for the tiny village of Lacroix-sur-Meuse in the Lorraine region of France. In August of 1944, when General George S. Patton's Third Army tanks thundered eastward toward the Rhine, I was the first American officer to enter Lacroix. I was not heading a combat command, but simply approached the village in a jeep driven by my French liaison officer whose in-laws resided there. He headed for their home, a great farmhouse at the edge of Lacroix, and as we drove down the main thoroughfare we were puzzled that no one came out to greet us. Then the reason became immediately and frighteningly apparent. As we rounded a corner by the main village hall, there in the middle of the street was a huge German Tiger tank, its crew resting in the turret. We did a screeching U-turn and beat an inglorious retreat down a dirt road and up a hillside where we watched through binoculars until we could see the tank head out of town in the direction of St. Mihiel. We made another reconnaissance and now the villagers were out in full force. *Les Boches sont partis!* ("The Germans have left!") they exulted, and the celebration began.

So fast had General Patton's forces moved through the Lorraine, that Lacroix and other nearby villages had been spared. That evening we dined with the French officer's mother and father-in-law and enjoyed a superb fondue made from the famous cheese of the region. Meat, of course, was out of the question as it, along with most other staples, had been requisitioned by the German troops. I learned then that the French do many things with food but one thing they won't do is serve cheese fondue to a party of one. Fondue is meant to be experienced by two people together. A solo act is practically unheard of.

A few years ago the dear old French couple who entertained me in 1944 were noting their 60th wedding anniversary and my wife and I were invited to attend. An important business engagement kept my bride from going and she insisted I go alone. So back I went into this citadel of love and cheese on my own. Rats! Here I was in the most romantic region of the most romantic country on earth. Dinnertime is the most romantic part of the day. All the pretty young couples huddle over tiny tables inside charming cafes, gazing deeply into each other's eyes—while eating cheese fondue.

In France, you get nothing to eat for breakfast except a roll. They call it *petit dejeuner*, but it's still a roll. For luncheon, if hiking through the spider-web roads that border the Meuse River, you get a sandwich, if you remember to stick one in your pocket. I didn't. All day I tramped through fields strewn with poppies, hungry as a Left Bank artist, sustained by the thought of fondue for dinner.

Lacroix-sur-Meuse is a tiny village and it has one of two country inns. I went to *Peche à la Truite*, where you can catch fat trout from a stocked stream and have them prepared as you wish. No trout for me, only fondue. I sat myself at a candle-lit-corner table. "Je regrette, Monsieur," said the waiter, "there is a two-person minimum for fondue."

Down one street and up the next, past postcard and tobacco shops. Always the same story. Two-person minimum. I was completely frustrated, so much so that I got in my rental car and drove 10 miles to St. Mihiel where I knew there were restaurants galore. To visit this section of *la belle France* and not eat fondue was unthinkable. Somewhere must be a bistro willing to serve fondue for one. Down a back alley I found a tiny restaurant with no one in it.

The place needed business. Yes, the waiter grudgingly said, he would serve fondue for one.

Oh boy! Oh boy! They brought the fondue. What a catastrophe! Fondue may be romantic for two. For one, it's a bigger flop than the Maginot line. You pick up the bread cube on the skinny fork and dip it in the bubbling pot of cheese. If it falls off the fork, the tradition goes, you have to give the other person a kiss. Under the circumstances there were grave difficulties in the plan. Eating fondue is a production number. Each tiny chunk must be dipped, twisted, allowed to cool—a lot of work for little food. It's something like eating artichokes. Consuming a two-portion pot of fondue takes one person twice as long. You fill up long before the pot empties out. The cheese turns brown and starts smoking. Out comes the waiter from the cubbyhole, snuffing the flame. Dinner is over.

Eating fondue alone at sunset in a charming French bistro overlooking the Meuse is the loneliest thing. Like dancing solo, it can be done but it's not much fun and you look absurd doing it. The French know love and they know good food, and the two-person fondue rule is well grounded on both points. With no one on the other side of the table, fondue is a pot of scalding goop and a long, silly fork and a basket full of stale bread. When it's gone, you don't have kisses on your mouth. What you have is pizza burn.

——◆◆——

Children Name Most Beloved, Most Hated Thanksgiving Foods

Children love Thanksgiving because it's a time of family togetherness and good eating, in addition to being a time to give thanks for the abundance we have. Some kids single out a specific food as their favorite on Thanksgiving, but at the same time, most kids can also point to a specific Thanksgiving Day treat that they can't stand. And so, in the interest of keeping the public informed on this crucial topic, we present a children's view of what they like and don't like at the Thanksgiving table. The following kids are from Margo Storey's third-grade class at the Mary E. Dardess Elementary School in Chatham.

At dinner, I like stuffing that my mom makes. The spices in it taste good, I also like it. My favorite Thanksgiving food is mashed potatoes. I like lots of gravy on my potatoes too. It is yummy. My grandmother makes them. I like them more than anything. The Thanksgiving food that I absolutely hate is escalloped oysters. They are yukky. They are mushy and soupy.

—*Lindsay A. Leal*

My favorite Thanksgiving food is dessert. My mom makes chocolate-covered peanut butter balls. They taste like Reese's Peanut Butter Cups. They are round with peanut butter on the inside and chocolate on the outside. I like them because they melt in your mouth so fast. I don't like Brussels sprouts. They look like tiny little green cabbages. I don't like them because they taste terrible. My dad is the only one who eats them!

—*Megan McGowan*

The best part of Thanksgiving is when I sit around the table and talk. My favorite food is chocolate mousse pie because I like sugar a lot. I like Cool Whip on my pie. I like it also because my mom and I make it together. The thing I don't like is carrot casserole. I don't like carrots for one thing, and I don't like casserole for the second thing!

—*Travis Burrows*

I like cranberry relish because it has cranberries, pineapples, oranges, apples and sugar in it. It's a nice shade of red. I also like to make it by grinding it up. I don't like stuffing at all, because bread, onions

164

and celery are in it. I hate them mixed up. Stuffing makes me feel like I'm going to throw up.

—*Liam Conway*

I like pumpkin pie because my Grandma and I make it together. I don't like boiled onions because they smell like my sister's socks.

—*Scott F. Purdue*

My favorite foods on Thanksgiving are mashed potatoes and stuffing. I like the mashed potatoes with a little puddle of gravy on top so that when I push my fork against the side of it, it runs down over the edge like a waterfall. I like the stuffing also, because my mom only makes it on Thanksgiving and Christmas, so it's special to me. The food I don't like very much are sweet potatoes. The reason I don't like sweet potatoes is because sometimes they're too sweet for me. I prefer sweet things for dessert. Yes and No potato!

—*Jean Nebesar*

I like squash at Thanksgiving the best because we pick it in the summer from the garden. My mother fries the squash. She puts sugar in it to make it sweet. I don't like beets. My sister Ashley says beets are hearts with blood around it. I don't like the taste.

—*Jessica Cunningham*

I like turkey the best. Turkey is the best because it is juicy. The skin is crispy. The food I don't like is cranberry sauce. It tastes like rotten purple blueberries.

—*Edward Ross*

I like turkey because it is juicy. When you put gravy on it and put it in your mouth it melts. It is my favorite. When we put stuffing in it, mmmm! Yes! I don't like yams. They taste like sickening, very sweet potatoes.

—*Monica Rose Meyer*

At Thanksgiving I don't like scalloped oysters. They smell stinky. The oysters are gooey and slimy. It looks like gray mush when it's all cooked. I love the turkey when it's all cooked. I love the turkey because it is juicy and yummy. I like when it's cooking because it smells so good. It's crispy and brown when it comes out of the oven.

—*Ben Witherell*

The Thanksgiving food I like is pumpkin pie. I like pumpkin pie because it is spicy and sweet. I feel happy when I eat pumpkin pie because I help make it. The Thanksgiving food I don't like is white potatoes because they are dry.

—*Laura Montag*

Turkey is my favorite food for our Thanksgiving feast. I like it because it tastes good, especially with gravy on it. I like it when it's crispy. Squash is my least favorite food that I have on Thanksgiving. I don't like the color of it, and it doesn't taste good to me.

—*Jessica Fox*

I like mashed potatoes for Thanksgiving because my mom and I peel them and cook them together. They are good! I like turkey because it's crispy fresh and good. I hate spinach because it's disgusting and my brother says gross things about it.

—*Jennifer Everetts*

I like turkey because it is juicy, tender, it melts in your mouth, and it tastes so good. The food I don't like is peas. They taste bad and they make me sick. They're too soft and mushy. I don't like how they feel in my mouth.

—*Erik O'Dell*

For Thanksgiving I like cranberry sauce because it tastes good. I usually will take several spoonfuls of it. I gobble it up fast. I don't like the turkey because it's dry. I don't think it tastes good either. It puts a horrible smelling steam in the air.

—*Christina Sauter*

Soon our house will be filled with the delicious smells of Thanksgiving. Most of them I like. Some I don't. My favorite food on Thanksgiving is mashed potatoes. They are salty, buttery and lumpy. They are smooth in my throat. I absolutely hate turnips! The worst part of them is their taste. They have a sharp bitter taste. They feel lumpy on my tongue. They smell like a rotten egg!

—*Matt Hover*

The food I like the most is the turkey because I help my mom cook it. The food I hate the most is the cranberry pie because my mom doesn't put sugar in it.

—*Tim Lyons*

I like turkey cause it's sliced thin. My mom cooks it very well with gravy on the top. The turkey that my mom makes has stuffing in it. Squash, my dad and I don't like. It's icky! I do not like squash cause it smells bad.

—*Elizabeth Brorup*

My favorite Thanksgiving food is turkey because it's good for me. I like it because it's the best food on the table, I think. The food I hate on Thanksgiving is squash because it tastes like pumpkin and I hate pumpkin.

—*Ryan Legere*

I like pumpkin pie because it is very moist. It has a taste that makes me feel good. It smells like a bite of pumpkin. I don't like turkey because it is hard for me to cut. I think it is very disgusting. I also think that it shouldn't have been invented.

—*Amanda Rogers*

I like Thanksgiving dinner because I like the smell of the turkey when it's cooking in the oven and it tastes so good. I like to make mountains out of the mashed potatoes. I put gravy into the middle of the potato mountains but I don't like the taste of potatoes.

—*Andrew J. Behrens*

On Thanksgiving I like turkey because it is good. I help my mom make the turkey. It is fun. On Thanksgiving I hate green beans because they are yucky tasting. My dad makes them.

—*Jen Mayer*

Titillating the Taste Buds

At this season of the year, after the long, hard winter of '93 our taste buds have waned into sluggishness. They need a jolt. Farm folks of yesteryear had a remedy for this. After winter months of overloading on sausage, ham hocks, pancakes, johnny cake, fried pork and other hearty victuals, their appetites were sort of "petered out."

It was about this time in April, when I lived on Payn Avenue, that my mother would send me over to the little brook that ran out of Borden's Pond. Armed with a shovel and a pail, I would search the stream banks until I found the green tendrils of that eye-watering, tonsil-twinging, liver-up-heaver . . . the lowly "hoss radish."

Don't mistake this homemade appetizer for those bottles of gray-colored pap sitting on the shelves in supermarkets. In addition to its culinary attributes, the Shakers dried it and sold it as a digestive. They also purveyed it as a relief for dropsy. For farm wives, who had a hankering for pickles, but were not able to digest those backfiring tasties, they scraped some horseradish into a bottle, added a little salt and enough vinegar to cover.

After a week or two on the kitchen shelf it was placed on the dinner table. One teaspoon would quickly dislodge and start moving through the digestive tract of staccato belching with machine gun regularity, plus a few hot tears.

It did not take long for me to find and dig out the long, white roots, and washing off the muck in the clear brook waters was no chore at all. The martyr's slot fell on the shoulders of my mother and our maid, Jennie Thompson, who peeled the roots, sliced them and forced them through a meat grinder. Holding a root so far away that their arm sockets creaked, they would take turns at the grater. In a minute their eyes started to water and tears welled down their cheeks. The fumes went up their nostrils. They choked and spluttered even though the kitchen windows and doors had been opened wide.

I remember one morning when our neighbor, "Chick" Rivenburgh, came to the back door, saw it open and started into the kitchen. He stopped dead in his tracks as if hit with a baseball bat. The sight of two weeping females, coughing and sniffling, assured him that a catastrophe had hit the house and he immediately withdrew.

The fumes filled the room.

Even Conrad, our old beagle hound who had sneaked in for a snooze behind the cook stove, staggered drunkenly to his feet and headed for the door and lurched out into the fresh air.

Jennie Thompson had presence of mind enough to throw a towel over the canary's cage and hustle him into the dining room. Even so, he was wobbling in his perch.

Later, Jennie recalled, "Sweetie Boy never sang a note for almost a month."

It was in April that our ever-remembered friend, George Stark, best recalled as Chatham's police chief and a loquacious auctioneer, would bottle vast quantities and peddle it house-to-house. George always implied it was an aphrodisiac and would whisper to the menfolk with a knowing worldly wink, "Good for what ails you." He also claimed he cleaned his false dentures by soaking them overnight in a bottle of the red hot root.

Even those in perfect health would find a small dose helpful when going out in the cold. Or, on having returned home from the field and shivering from a chill, they would soon be all aglow after taking one or two teaspoons in a little hot water.

For the modern palate perhaps not accustomed to such fiery condiments, we suggest the following:

Horseradish Cream

Beat 1/2 cup heavy cream

Stir in 1/2 teaspoon salt and a few grains of cayenne

Add 2–4 tablespoons of freshly grated horseradish and four teaspoons of vinegar.

For a milder taste, omit the vinegar, add 1/2 teaspoon Dijon mustard and 3 tablespoons mayonnaise.

——⊰◆⊱——

Some Means of Wetting Your Whistle

Now that we are expecting the hot, humid days of the seventh month, who remembers a wonderfully refreshing summer drink called "Switchel"? In this corner last week, in recalling haying time on yesteryear's farms, I mentioned that farmers carried jugs of switchel into the fields as a cooling libation. Several of my readers wanted to know more about this thirst quencher, so here's the story.

Switchel is a mixture of molasses, ginger and cold spring water poured into a brown jug. Set in some shady corner of a stone wall, it slaked the parched throat of many a stripling farm lad while "pitchin' on" hay. Hard cider was for the older folks. As a young teen-ager, working on the Kelly farm in East Chatham, by mistake (or with intent) I took a long swig of hard cider. Not many minutes later, I was picked up from the ground having slithered off a load of hay and dragged under a tree. Joe Kelly, for whom I worked that summer, thought it was sunstroke, but his sister, Mary, a devout

Roman Catholic, crossed herself when she saw me. "It's his first encounter with Satan," she said.

Raspberry and currant shrub, it was called. It made a very cooling summer drink diluted with well water. The gentle and refined old lady who made it in the kitchen of her Seven Bridges Road home near Old Chatham has long since departed from her berry patch. Wearing mitts to protect her hands from the briars and a large hat to protect her wondrous complexion, she reminded one of a Gainsborough duchess.

It was supposed to be a harmless enough beverage offered to the dominie or other important guests when calling. But one day her neighbors found her flat on the ground in the currant bushes, hands fluttering, very pink of cheek and a loosened braid hanging down her back. "I guess she took too much this time," they whispered as they carried her into the house.

Bob Lank, who served for many years as postmaster of Malden Bridge, brewed up another long-forgotten refresher. Welsh in origin, it was called "metheglin." The English called it "meade." Bob found the recipe for this libation among his grandfather's papers. As far as we could determine, parts of rain water and honey were distilled in some mysterious fashion, put into bottles and laid away in the cellar, where time and the darkness had its way in the mellowing process.

The post office in Malden Bridge was exceedingly hot in the early 1950s, so Bob, who enjoyed the fruit of the grape, brought a musty bottle of metheglin to work. He took a few swigs before sorting the morning mail and a few more licks as the day progressed. When postal patrons arrived, they found everyone else's mail in their boxes and Bob sitting in a chair stiffer than a stake. His eyes were always crossed, but this day his orbs were almost attached to his nose and his face was wreathed with a perpetual smile. By 3 P.M. some good

Samaritan locked up the post office and drove the postmaster and his metheglin home.

The cream-colored umbrella-like flowers of the elderberry bushes are in blossom along the roadsides. The flowers make a delicious sparkling white wine. At meetings of the church Ladies Aid Society it would be served with a slab of pound cake. A treat long to be remembered, it would loosen the tongue of anyone who might be shy in speaking. The late Ida Thorn recalled a meeting of the Ladies of the Old Chatham Methodist Church. One prim matron, who hadn't said a word during the entire meeting, put down her third glass of elderberry wine on the table and suddenly announced, "Our cat ate up two of her kittens this morning."

No one I know makes homemade root beer any more. A bottle of Hire's extract and a yeast cake mixed with cold water. A large dish of homemade vanilla ice cream with a glass of root beer was a Sunday treat.

Referring to last week's column on haying, Mary Lester of New Lebanon recalls that "aftermath," or the second cutting of hay from a field, was also called "rowan." One of your younger readers asks, "Why do you write of the past and not the future or the present?" For the same reason many people are using kerosene lamps again, or buying hand-cranked ice cream freezers and thinking of the days when they were young and permitted to lick the dasher. Possibly it's nostalgia or old age, but it seems the time of youth is happier and certainly more secure than in later life.

Apples—Nature's Bounty

Every farmstand throughout the countryside these autumnal days is filled with nature's bounty—ripe, red apples. The apple is cultivated in strange and innumerable varieties throughout the world and in our day-to-day conversations the word *apple* frequently appears. As a youth, I was fascinated by the term *Adam's apple*. Back in the early 1930s, a Mr. Frank Tabor was the director of the Morris Memorial. He had a magnificent Adam's apple that slid up and down his throat while eating or drinking. We know that Adam and Eve lost their lease on Eden because of an apple—there's Adam's apple again—and Shakespeare has Macbeth describe someone as "A goodly apple, rotten at the core." The orb in the Royal British regalia is in the form of an apple, and how often have we said, "He was the apple of her eye"? An "apple pie bed" is one made in such a manner that it is impossible to straighten one's legs.

Last week, having built up an urge for apples, we approached the fruit section of our local supermarket. There were rows on rows of brightly polished apples in various shades of yellow, green and red. Two kindly ladies next to me were discussing the varieties and which ones they would choose for baking, for pies, for applesauce, *ad infinitum*. There was a time long ago when quantities of this most delicious fruit were stored in the farmhouse cellar during the winter months. Usually there were at least four or five barrels.

Two or three would be Greenings which were used for pies, turnovers, Brown Bettys and applesauce. The McIntoshes, Sheep's Nose and Seek-No-Furthers were for eating. The early summer apples were already in Mason jars, sitting primly on the shelves next to the rows of crab-apple jelly. In a far corner was a barrel or two of hard cider, fermenting peacefully and waiting for the moment when someone would turn the spigot and fill the pitcher. Next to it was the vinegar barrel to which had been added the "mother," a mucilaginous substance taken from last year's barrel; a most necessary procedure in good vinegar making.

Just before bedtime the children carried a kerosene lantern and milk pan down the creaky cellar stairs. The temperature was just right for preserving the apples. As they took apples from a barrel and filled the milk pan, they were frightened momentarily as a rat skittered out of the darkness and disappeared into a foundation hole. Returning upstairs, the family sat about the kitchen table in the soft, golden glow of lamplight and here they peeled and munched two or three apples before retiring.

Are there any of you dear readers who recall eating the reddish brown Russet or the crunchy Sheep's Nose? What housewife has time these days to make a pan dowdy? Years ago, the well beloved Marion Van Ness gave me a recipe: To three quarts of apples pared and cored, add one cupful of sugar, grated nutmeg, one cupful of water and butter the size of a walnut. Put in an earthenware or glass pie plate and cover it with an inch-thick pie crust. Bake slowly for two and a half hours, then serve it with generous helpings of thick cream and sugar. Heaven!

In 1840, when Martin van Buren had, during four years as president, become enamored of foreign elegance and filled the White House with exquisite possessions from across the seas, the prospects for his election looked bright. The Whig Party sought desperately for a satisfactory candidate to oppose Van Buren, a Democrat, but finding none, finally settled on an elderly general, William Henry Harrison, a hero of the War of 1812. Van Buren might easily have won reelection had it not been for the American apple. A journalist supporter of "Little Van" printed a contemptuous canard to the effect that if "Old Tippecanoe [Harrison] were subsidized by a pension of $2,000 and given a barrel of fermented apple juice, he would prefer his cabin to the White House."

At once the conflict was joined between the backers of a president who wore "ruffled shirts and silken hose" and the plain folk who stood for "log cabins and hard cider." Harrison's supporters formed Log Cabin Clubs and, in some instances, log cabins were built where hard cider was served lavishly. Choruses of raucous male voices joined in singing about Harrison, the plain dirt farmer of Indiana where lay the bones of Johnny Appleseed.

> Upon his board there ne'er appeared
> The costly sparkling wine,
> But plain hard cider such as cheered
> In days of auld lang syne.

Torchlights illuminated countless Main Streets throughout the nation. The Whigs shouted "OK, OK, Old Kinderhook!" The parading Democrats sang out:

> Let Van from his silver drink wine
> And lounge on his cushioned settee.
> Our man on his buckeye couch can recline
> Content with hard cider is he.

Van Buren lost his reelection bid and retired to Lindenwald where he became a gentleman farmer, and among other things, raised bumper crops of apples.

―――――⟫•⟪―――――

Half a Loaf Can Be Worse Than One

There's something scary about a blob of bread dough. It's alive, like the stuff in the Steve McQueen movie. It's hard to figure how something so ghastly won its billing as the staff of life.

Good amateur bread bakers are a rarity. The very best in my book is Albert R. Douglas of the Upper Rayville Douglases, who has been turning out loaves of absolutely delicious French bread for aeons. Crusty brown on the outside and light as a feather on the inner portion, no better gift could anyone receive than a few hot loaves of Doug's bread to be slathered with butter and enjoyed with a good cheese and green salad.

I have watched Doug demonstrate his culinary prowess, and it always looked so perfectly simple. Granted, he does dust himself and the kitchen with a blizzard of flour, but what matter?

If Albert Douglas can perform this baking wizardry, why can't I? So I baked a loaf the other day to remind myself why I don't do it more often. Bread is the only food that is dead when you start making it, comes to life before your eyes, then must be killed off at high temperature before you can eat it. It's not food for the faint of heart.

Bread is harder to make than cake, without tasting as good. The better the bread, the faster it goes bad. Bread is bubbly with a short shelf life, something like newspapers. I never would have made it but for the food processor. The machine was feeling lonely. My bride, after craving it so badly in the heady days of food processors, had cast it aside. Women have been known to treat objects of their affection that way. How may crock pots and hot-air corn poppers have been sacrificed to the altar of Sr. Vincent de Paul to make room for the next appliance?

So I felt sorry for the food processor. Its days were numbered unless I took action. Maybe there was a foodstuff around the house that needed processing.

"Why don't you process some bread?" my wife said. "I read in a magazine that women can't resist men who bake bread." (Aha, that's why Albert Douglas is always surrounded by a bevy of beauties.) I, too, shall have the ladies seeking me out—so I started processing.

I processed the flour. I processed the salt and the nonfat dry milk. Then it was time for The Packet. There are countless sleepy organisms inside each packet, waiting, waiting for their sugar and warm water. Waiting for the chance to start bubbling and foaming and multiplying.

I brought them to life with a flick of the wooden spoon. They were insatiable. They devoured the sugar and wanted more. *The Joy of Cooking* told the whole, terrible story.

"Yeasts are living organisms with 3.2 million cells to the pound and not one is exactly like the other," the book said. There were more living, breathing yeasts spinning around on the ball of dough inside the processor than were people on the face of the earth! Like people, each was a unique individual. Around and around they went on the whirling orb, blindly feeding their faces.

I watched the blob rise. First it was the size of a softball. Then it grew to the size of a cabbage head. Then it swelled to the size of a melon. It was horrible to behold. It had to be stopped, I jammed the unwieldy blob into the bread pan. It fought back, sticking to my fingers.

Please don't do it, said billions of living organisms, not one of which was exactly like any other.

Into the oven they went just the same. The dial said 375 degrees. It was better this way.

Half an hour later the bread was done. It was flat and tough, a complete failure. What went wrong? The book had the answer for that, too. "If allowed to expand, yeast dough can use up its energy," *The Joy of Cooking* explained, "In this case, there is little rising power left for the baking period, when it is most needed."

It seems I was too soft on the yeasts. I should have killed them much earlier. I'm just a nice, sensitive guy, the kind who bakes bread. My dearest and I ate the bread, slowly. Perhaps women can't resist men who bake bread, but they can resist the bread.

⎯⎯⎯▷◆◁⎯⎯⎯

A Harried Scramble for a Column

I always enjoy reading "Page 6" in the *New York Post*. The page is filled with gossipy tidbits, and one item caught my eye. The *Post* reported that, in Gotham, Donald Trump always eats scrambled eggs for luncheon at La Grenouille, and this interested me for three reasons. I am very fond of scrambled eggs. I am not very fond of Donald Trump. The owner of the fashionable restaurant where he dines is Giselle Masson, who with her late husband Paul Masson, operated Les Pyrenees Restaurant in Canaan during the early 1950s.

Now back to scrambled eggs. On his dining choice, Trump says, "It's the easiest and safest thing to prepare." This space begs to disagree. In fact it is very easy to make bad scrambled eggs. I have seen it done hundreds of times. I have often been required to eat eggs that have been improperly scrambled by normally fine cooks. There are entire nations that have never learned how to scramble eggs. One only has to travel to Great Britain. The farther north one goes, the more out of touch with acceptable scrambling techniques the native populace becomes.

For a few months during World War II, I was on temporary duty in Dartmouth, England. I was billeted with a wonderful English couple, and I shared with them the rations I was allotted. Next to Adolf Hitler, the worst thing to come of that war was powdered eggs. No matter how they were prepared, they always tasted like chopped up cardboard.

It was my good fortune to befriend a supply sergeant in a nearby Quartermaster Corps depot who could provide me with fresh eggs. The British supply of fresh eggs for civilians was almost non-existent as eggs were going to the armed forces. My hosts in Dartmouth, Charles and Mary Brighton, were exultant when I brought to their kitchen a dozen shiny, white eggs.

Mary suggested we have some the next morning for breakfast— scrambled. After the army's scrambled eggs served in a cold mess kit, this would be a special treat for me as well. I went to bed that night dreaming of moist, warm, almost frothy scrambled eggs served with a rasher of bacon, which I also would provide.

Mary busied herself in the kitchen and then, with a flourish, set the plate before me. The scrambled eggs were pale pellets! They tended to roll around the plate like marbles. I enjoy the clatter of a good egg as well as the next person, but the noise created when a single adamantine sphere of egg fell off a fork was enough to stop conversation. The eggs were served with tomatoes that had seemingly been broiled the week before and left to mellow in the harsh winds sweeping over the Devonshire moors.

They resembled eggs that might have been dug up from a peat bog, the last lunch of a Bronze Age hunter overtaken by unfortunate circumstance. The tomatoes, in any case, were better than the eggs.

Wherever the British have colonized, they have taken their appalling scrambling techniques. This is because all true English persons like soft-boiled eggs surrounded by so many ritual artifacts that they take a full hour to consume. Scrambling is thus seen as a bitter necessity. They don't even use the word *scramble*. I think the word is disgusting.

"Give us some disgusting eggs, love," one of our British cousins will say. This from a culture that has given us such distinguished food names as "toad-in-the-hole," "pigs in blankets" and "spotted dick."

We don't even speak of France where scrambled eggs are no more than an undercooked gelatinous mass.

In Mexico what they do is incomprehensible!

"Huevos rancheros"—eggs prepared with fiery jalapeno peppers—are enough to destroy the digestive system permanently. The Mexicans also serve eggs with pasta for breakfast. They cook the eggs for nine hours until all the moisture is removed, then they cozy them up to thick, chewy noodles.

The noodles come with watery tomato sauce that leaks into the eggs, moistening them and causing them to change color. The unwary breakfaster is visited by the uneasy feeling that an emetic child, a junior member of the kitchen staff, has cut his finger moments before bringing in the plate.

Not that I mean to suggest that the scrambled eggs of the United States are entirely blameless. Here the problem is different—too much moisture rather than too little. Often in the USA, eggs are scrambled in a pan that has been used to prepare 905 pounds of bacon. The grease has not been completely poured out. The eggs thus swim in a giant ocean of animal fat to a point where they look like the last bathers in a badly polluted municipal plunge. The eggs are not so much cooked as pushed around and gathered up. The spatula holding them drips profusely as the eggs are transferred to the plate.

If a way could be found to wring them out, these eggs could supply enough lubricant to satisfy the needs of a small auto repair shop for a week. None of that happened at La Grenouille, I'm certain of that. It seems clear that Donald Trump will never have to deal with badly scrambled eggs. But he should know that there are eight million eggs in the naked city, many of them heading for a bad end.

━━➤◆⟞━━

August—and Corn Is King

When I first started to investigate corn I was overwhelmed by the sheer volume of information available. Corn, after all, has been around for nearly 10 thousand years, with origins in southern Mexico and Central America. Its progenitor may have been a variety of wild corn only a couple of inches long, which may have been domesticated and gradually enlarged to the size we now know. But this is mere speculation, and distinguished careers have been spent arguing the origin of corn. The one thing experts do agree upon is how corn should be eaten—just cooked on the cob with plenty of butter.

Now that it's August, corn is king and for our money, Columbia County produces some of the nation's best corn. The summer's cool, damp weather has produced a splendid crop, and for the next few weeks we look forward to enjoying row after row of pearly kernels. What is the best way to eat corn? Regardless of facial contortions, butter from mouth to ear and greasy fingers, most of us prefer "gnawing" it from the cob shark-wise. Toothless elders and delicate ladies choose to slice the kernels off, but the taste and guzzling sounds are missing. It takes courage and finesse to attack an ear in public and it is thus best enjoyed at the home table.

The recipes for preparing corn are, however, varied and all of them delicious. There are, however, certain rules for boiling corn on the cob that must be followed. Lucky are those who can dash to the garden, snap off the ears, strip off the husks and silk and in less than five minutes drop them in a kettle half-filled with roiling boiling water. Never add salt. It toughens the kernels, but do add a tablespoon of sugar. Bring the water to a second boil and cook from five to seven minutes, depending on the age of the corn.

On the farm, succotash was a favorite dish, but it seems to be fading from our menus. Early settlers learned to make this warming dish from the Indians. Times have long since vanished when the housewife could go to the milk house in the morning and skim off a quart of heavy cream from last night's milking. Tender fresh young lima beans were cooked and added to the kernels, which had been scraped from the cob and simmered until tender. Several bits of salt pork and diced green pepper would be added and, after draining off the water, the heavy, rich cream would be added, along with seasonings, to the corn-bean mixture.

Many of the families (sometimes referred to as "Bushwhackers") who lived in isolated areas of Gallatin and Taghkanic helped ease their rugged lives with corn "likker." The county sheriff would often be summoned to shut down a still hidden in the deep woods. Infrequently, travelers from the "outside world" would be invited by these shy people to "sit a spell." Usually the visitor would sit longer than a spell since he was unable to stand after consuming a gourd of the clear liquid with the kick of a mule. While the visitor would depart with a throbbing head, the distiller would repair to his corn husk mattress and a good night's sleep.

The Mount Lebanon Shakers raised a variety known as "broom corn" and from it developed a thriving trade from selling seed and making the first flat house brooms. So whether it be corn pone, corn sticks, fritters, creamed or on the cob—go to it while the going is good.

Finally, here is a recipe for what the Shakers called 'CORN OYSTERS'

2 ears corn, shucked*

1 teaspoon milk

2 tablespoons sifted flour

1 large egg, separated

1 tablespoon shortening

1 tablespoon unsalted butter

In a bowl, combine corn, flour, pepper, egg yolk and salt to taste. Stir until combined.

In a small bowl beat egg white until it stiffens, then fold into corn mixture. In a large skillet, heat shortening and butter over moderate heat until hot but not smoking. In the fat, cook heaping tablespoons of corn mixture until they are golden brown. Keep oysters warm in a 200 degree oven. Makes about 10 oysters.

*If the corn is not milky, add the milk.

⪼◆⪻

Chicken à la King

Famous dish not named for royalty, but former
New Lebanon hotel owner

If one looks at the menu in most restaurants today there will be found a delectable dish called "Chicken à la King." Not only is it served throughout the world, but so popular has it become that a canned variety can be found on most grocer's shelves. It may be assumed that the dish was given its name because at some time or other it tickled the palate of a reigning monarch, who was a devotee of good food. This is far from correct. It was named in honor of E. Clark King, a native of the Lebanon Valley, who sleeps today in the cemetery of the Evergreens in Lebanon Springs.

Mr. King was born in a rambling structure on Cemetery Road, known for many years as the Parker House. At an early age, after receiving his education in New Lebanon schools, King left the Valley and entered the hotel field. From menial employment, his success was rapid and in the early 1900s, he became the owner of the Brighton Beach Hotel, not far from Coney Island. This was a popular resort in the summer months and guests came by the score to enjoy the excellent meals, the commodious rooms and the fresh sea breezes off the Atlantic Ocean. One of the hotel's chief attractions was a long dining room which faced the ocean and which, on a warm summer's evening, was a most pleasant place to dine and relax after a delectable repast.

One July evening while Mr. and Mrs. King were enjoying their dinner, the maitre d' brought them a dish that was not on the menu and one that proved to be a gastronomic surprise. It apparently had as its base diced chicken and to it had been added cream, shredded green pepper, onion juice, mushrooms and paprika. The Kings were advised that the hotel's chef, George Greenwald, had prepared only enough for one serving. But the next evening, on the dinner menu, there was a new item served at the Brighton Beach Hotel—"Chicken à la King, $1.25."

Thus, the famous dish was born and another link with Columbia County was established. The late W. Gordon Cox of Old Chatham once recalled a visit to the Brighton Beach Hotel as a boy to spend a week or two with the King's son, Clark, Jr. One of the youngsters' delights was a visit to Coney Island but, before leaving, they were advised by the elder King that they must come home by 11 P.M.

Engrossed in the many attractions of the celebrated resort, they lost all sense of time, but, to their constant surprise, if they weren't on the way by the appointed hour, a bell boy from the hotel would emerge from the crowd, tap them on the shoulder, and remind them it was after 11.

Mr. Cox was puzzled how the bellboy could find two small boys in the vast throngs of people, and always at the right moment. Years later, he discovered the secret. Mr. King had a hotel house detective follow the young pair each evening and, at the hour of 11, the bellboy would locate the detective who had followed the boys. The bellboy's search was not difficult after that.

Mr. King is recalled as a jovial person, good natured, an ideal hotel proprietor, and one whose death was greatly mourned in 1936. But though he has long gone to his rest, the dish that was named for E. Clark King is still among America's favorites. The original recipe of Chef George Greenwald has been preserved and amateur chefs can prepare it, the same as it was served at the old Brighton Beach Hotel.

CHICKEN À LA KING

Melt two tablespoons of butter in a saucepan and sauté one half a diced green pepper followed by one cup thinly sliced mushrooms. Stir and cook five minutes and then add two level tablespoons of flour and a half teaspoon of salt. Cook until frothy, stirring continually. Add one pint of cream and continue to stir until the sauce thickens. Pour sauce, peppers and mushrooms into a double boiler. Add three cups of heavily diced chicken and mix well, allowing it to become very hot.

In a separate saucepan, melt a quarter cup of butter and beat in the yolks of three eggs, one teaspoon of lemon juice, and one half teaspoon of paprika. Stir this mixture until it thickens a little and then combine with the chicken mixture. Add sherry and slivered pimiento before serving on toast points or rice.

The Case of the Disappearing Desserts

SAN MIGUEL DE ALLENDE—For dessert lovers, Mexico is absolute heaven on earth. One of my favorite restaurants here is Pepe's Patio where, on Sundays, a bountiful buffet is served topped off by a table groaning with *postres* (desserts) served in an all-you-can-eat basis. Pepe's is no place for calorie counters. Can you imagine how many calories there are in a huge slice of moist, dark Black Forest cake, or golden peanut butter flan, or a symphony of mousse—mango, Kahlua, rum eggnog? How about *Torta de Cielo* (Heavenly Torte), Pepe's chiffon cake almond pudding—all topped off with a galaxy of ice creams so rich and heavy they make similar offerings in the States look like pap.

At lunch the other day at Pepe's, someone wondered whatever became of baked Alaska, once considered the ultimate in classy desserts, way back in the days before *crème brulée.* This led to someone else inquiring into the whereabouts of cherries jubilee, which you don't hear a lot about anymore—not even restaurants that allegedly cater to "classic American cuisine." A place like Pepe's wouldn't be caught dead serving up cherries jubilee or "baked Alaska" or more humble traditional dishes of stuff like heavenly hash or "ambrosia." When was the last time you saw angel food cake with chocolate icing on a menu?

My private source here for angel food cake is a *panaderia* (bakery) redolent with the fragrance of freshly baked goods. Their version of angel food cake is so nostalgic, that it's become my Proustian madeleine. One bite—one whiff—and I'm wafted back to my

12th birthday party when my mother entered the dining room lofting an angel cake ablaze with candles.

Last year while dining in New York, I finally mustered the nerve to order a baked Alaska (my first pseudo-gourmet gesture). It turned out to be a major disappointment, like the first kiss.

Flaming ice-cream isn't as great as it sounds and hardly worth the weird stares and snickers one must endure from curious onlookers as the thing is carried in. Watching it being carted in, borne aloft by a triumphant waiter, is by far the best part. Crepes Suzette haven't been heard from in quite a while, nor chocolate fondue. The era of the gaudy flaming desserts is pretty much over. Only bananas Foster survive, living on borrowed time at Brennan's in New Orleans.

There's probably not much call these days, I would imagine, for steak Diane—i.e., steak flambé. "Flambé" is too wonderful a word to be retired.

The most thrilling steak Diane I ever saw was served years ago at Albany's Golden Fox restaurant. An English friend ordered the steak and kept insisting the waiter add more brandy to flame the filet of beef. More liquor was poured on and when ignited, looked like a miniature Kuwaiti oil well completely involved in fire. The waiter who was preparing the dish looked nervously about as the flaming brandy spilled on the table and soon the tablecloth was afire. The flames were now glorious and ignited nearby window drapes. As we fled the table, the Englishman ordered loudly, "Now be careful, I don't want it overdone." A week later, the Golden Fox closed its doors forever. No wonder! I've been served nothing truly death-defying in flambéed dishes, since that memorable steak Diane. Sizzling rice soup and Mexican fajitas notwithstanding.

Whatever happened to good old lobster thermidor? It sounds intimidating, whatever it may be. It isn't dessert, but how did it vanish overnight about 15 years ago without a trace?

Actually, I think Jack's Restaurant in Albany has a crab thermidor on its menu, but I suspect they only keep it there to please old-timers who once enjoyed the delicacy at Keeler's. I can't imagine anyone's ordered it since 1973.

Does anybody still make trifle with lady fingers? (Do they still make lady fingers?) And whatever became of Jell-O cubes with Cool Whip and grasshopper pie with crushed Oreo cookie crumbs? While we're on the trail of the vanishing dessert, where might one locate a decent dish of rice pudding these days? With raisins—black ones, not yellow—and not too creamy? The Columbia Diner in Hudson makes a fair version, but it's really custard with rice, not the real McCoy, à la Nestletown Teahouse in Rider's Mills circa 1930.

Someone should open a place called "Mommy's" that would make tuna casseroles, open-faced peanut butter and jelly sandwiches, milk toast, baked beans, creamed eggs on toast and chicken pot pie. The bar would serve cocoa (with bobbing mini-marshmallows), lime phosphates, cherry cokes and chocolate milk, with such bar snacks as cream cheese-filled celery stalks and split wieners stuffed with Cheez Whiz.

Another thing I miss is cinnamon toast, one of life's major underrated treasures. The last piece of cinnamon toast I had was at the Desmond Americana in Albany. I slipped into the Desmond dining room and pretended I was staying there and grandly ordered a side of cinnamon toast. Whenever you find cinnamon toast on a menu—usually on some roadside coffee shop—they simply stick bread in a toaster and sprinkle sugar and cinnamon on top rather than broiling it until the cinnamon forms a nice thick, brown lavalike crust. If the Frugal Gourmet is so hot, let's see him knock out a classic order of cinnamon toast sometime; maybe he could get the recipe from the Desmond's chef, Michael St. John.

BRIGHT LIGHTS

The First Time I Saw Paris

Fifty-eight years ago this month, American and French forces liberated the city of Paris and in doing so, touched off one of the wildest celebrations of all time. At the time, I was a 25-year-old-captain serving in General George S. Patton's Third U.S. Army staff. Patton's command post (code name "Lucky Forward") was in Pithivier, some 60 miles south of Paris. This week I found a letter written to my family in August 1944. It reads as follows:

SOMEWHERE IN FRANCE

"As in the last war, Paris was the mecca of every soldier, and I can assure you the same holds true of World War II. I took "French leave" when we heard Paris was to be liberated and with my friend Lt. Oliver Burglund, a former Firestone tire executive, who had resided for several years in Paris, we headed north toward the city. As we approached, the road was filled with trucks bringing foodstuff to the city and yet there were hundreds of people on bicycles (we became used to that) pedaling into the countryside in search of edibles. We entered the city through the Porte d'Orleans and passed by the cathedral of Notre Dame which was filled with Parisians expressing gratitude for their liberation. Outside the age-old cloisters, kids were seeking to exchange postcards for gum and candy. All seemed to be quite hungry for anything to eat. Burglund then took me on a Cook's tour—the Eiffel Tower, the Arc de Triomphe, the place de la Concorde and taking lots of photographs in real tourist fashion. Our next stop was the Café de la Paix where we sat at a sidewalk table and watched as seemingly all of Paris passed by.

"The city is so exciting and so gay. I thought of all I had read and heard about it in story and song and here it was before my very eyes like a giant carnival. The streets were full of French soldiers but few Americans, so we were greeted with spontaneous, sincere welcomes wherever we went. At one point in the afternoon an American armored unit roared down the Champs Elysees which prompted an old Frenchman to make this sage comment: 'You have not an army but a huge factory on wheels.'

"We hopped in the jeep and drove to the Bois de Boulogne but we were halted by a French military unit who advised us to stop as there were still snipers in the woods. Back into the city and in the place de la Concorde was a burned out German tank. The tank symbolized the oppression wrought by the Nazis and each Frenchman as he passed the charred chassis either spit on it or performed other duties of nature on its blackened armor. C'est Paris!

"Seemingly everyone rode bicycles and what very few cars we saw would stridently peep-peep their horns adding to the general din. Some vehicles we saw were propelled by a Rube Goldberg device that looked like a charcoal burner and flumes of smoke poured out from the various orifices. As far as the bicycle traffic the man usually drove with his lady straddled over the rear fender. One very dignified looking couple were amusing, he in a blue homburg cutaway and winged collar, and she in a mink jacket and nifty little French bonnet perched over one eye; he pumping for all he was worth and she riding side saddle, but looking as dignified as if occupying the plush interior of a Rolls-Royce.

"Then, too, the lovely young women riding along with their skirts flying up to their midriffs, the Parisians not giving them a tumble but Burglund and I nearly wrecked the Jeep when a lovely expanse of limb and lacy underthings or none at all would flash by in a lovely vision of femininity. The women, for the most part, are tall, wasp-waisted, broad-shouldered and wear severely tailored clothes that accent the slimness of their waists. All wear wedgees, shoes with thick wooden soles that accent their height. Many carry slim umbrellas and they have gone in for platinum blonde upswept hairdos and from our sidewalk advantage we admired their queenly graceful stride. All this sounds like something from a man who had not seen a pretty woman since we debarked in Normandy. And that's perfectly true!

"The day was drawing to a close as we found a parking spot on the Rue Madeleine. Burglund wanted to find one of his favorite watering holes, Le Capricorn, and there it was. We entered a darkened lounge where a pianist in the corner was playing 'Manhattan Serenade,' and coupled with the subdued chatter of the patrons, the cigarette smoke, and the ambiance seemed to transplant me right back to the Stork Club or 21, it was so much like any smart Gotham supper club. We felt a bit out of place in our dusty OD uniforms, a piece of parachute silk about the neck and .30 revolvers in shoulder holsters. A young Frenchman invited us to join him and his wife in an aperitif. We thought white and red wine, but no, 'I can serve you Johnny Walker Black or Red Label. We have everything, what's your pleasure?'

"He was the owner of the club, has been in the U.S. many times, spoke perfect English and insisted we be his guests. He told us when the Germans invaded Paris he had sealed up his best wines and whiskeys behind a false wall which he opened this morning for the first time in four years. Later we were joined by his most attractive daughter and it was off to Le Club Badinage which could have been a 52nd Street hot spot with 'le jazz hot.' As we came through the door, the band swung into 'Sweet Georgia Brown' and topped it with a ragged rendition of 'the Star Spangled Banner' We were the only Americans present and cheers echoed from the walls.

"That night we drove back to the Champs-Elysées with the ladies perched on the Jeep's front fender, forging our way through tumultuous crowds of merry makers. Out hosts kindly provided us with a place to lay our weary heads and then our short leave was nearing its end. A light rain was beginning to fall, the streets glistened and there was the never-to-be-forgotten sight of three gorgeous young ladies—a blonde, a redhead and a brunette, one in fiery red, one in royal blue and the tall brunette in pure white, a triumvirate of colorful patriots walking arm-in-arm. You see, for years, the Germans would not permit the national colors to be displayed and now the tri-colors are everywhere.

"In retrospect, Burglund confirmed he could see not an iota of change in the city now engulfed in a colorful, majestic pageantry of gaiety after years of oppression, hardship and starvation. The spirit of the French has not been broken, far from it and the city itself is unmarked by the ravages of war. As we drove southward along the Seine, I felt as untold numbers of others have in the past . . . 'I'm in love with Paris.'"

≡►♦◄═══

The Greatest of Them All
Harry Howard's Name Is Enshrined for Prosperity in Columbia County and Little Old New York

Columbia County's volunteer firemen have always taken great pride in the beautiful Firemen's Home and Hospital at Hudson, but probably only a handful know the story of the man who gave the first subscription for this institution. Every good fireman, no matter where he resides, is dedicated to saving life and property and for that he is honored and held in the highest regard by his neighbors and business associates.

Probably no fireman, however, in the long history of fire fighting in the Empire State was more revered than a gallant, mustachioed leader of New York City's volunteer firemen in the mid-19th century.

His name has been enshrined in perpetuity on Columbia County soil, for the highway leading to the Firemen's Home from the City of Hudson has been named Harry Howard Avenue, for this member of the firemanic hall of fame. Harry Howard was born a foundling in New York City in 1824 and was adopted by a family named Howard. From his earliest youth he was a fire "buff" and joined a volunteer unit at the age of 15.

In the colorful days of firefighting in old New York, the units were given picturesque and often humorous names. Harry Howard joined Chatham Engine Co. No. 15, known as "the Wreath of Roses," and served first as a runner and then as a fireman. All apparatus in those days was hand-drawn and great was the competition between hose companies to reach a conflagration before a rival unit. A fire in downtown New York in what is now Greenwich Village would bring forth companies with such delightful sobriquets as "the Fly-By-Nights," "the Deadly Aces" or "Old Maids' Boys."

Chatham Engine Co. No. 15 quickly recognized the unusual young man in Harry Howard and he was quickly advanced to foreman, and in 1850, was elected assistant engineer. His unit operated in the present area of Chatham Square on the lower east side of Manhattan and thus took its name. Firemanic historians of the city have written much of Harry Howard. His powerful stride, his strident voice echoing through a voice trumpet over the roar of flames, his absolute disregard for personal safety to insure that his own men were not endangered made him a public hero second to none. He was beau ideal of the boys in the lower wards of the city. His dashing appearance and flowing Edwardian mustache were copied by the dandies of the day who looked upon Harry Howard as a Victorian superman. In 1857, at the age of 32, he was named chief of the New York City volunteer units. This was unprecedented, for at this rather tender age, young Howard was given the command of 51 engine companies, 61 hose companies numbering more than 5,000 men in their ranks.

On December 15, 1858, following a particularly disastrous fire, Chief Howard was presented a special certificate of merit by the City of New York for his role in saving the life of a fireman trapped in a blazing building. For the next two years he drove himself to utmost capacity, always leading his fire fighters to the very edge of the flames, and when the hand-pulled engines lagged, it was Chief Howard who like a cavalry officer brandishing his sword would urge volunteers on to greater speed. By this time every youngster and maiden in New York could easily recognize the handsome face of Chief Harry Howard in the newspapers more readily than they did the mayor of the city.

It is said by those who have recorded his life span, that Harry Howard was disappointed in love as a youth and he turned with a passion to fire fighting to quench the flames of love of the woman who spurned his affection.

In the summer of 1860, while leading a fire call to Grand Street, residents of New York cheered the man in the white helmet who led company after company to the scene of the blaze. Approaching the flames and while calling orders back over his shoulder to his followers, Chief Howard suddenly crumpled and rolled over on the pavement. Medical examination at the city hospital showed the great man had suffered a stroke, and the long striding legs which could cover a city block in a matter of seconds were now paralyzed for life.

New York City went almost into mourning when it learned this magnificent leader, whose personal enthusiasm had brought the city's fire units to unparalleled heights, would no longer cut a dashing figure through the streets. For the next 34 years, Harry Howard lived quietly in his beloved city watching the apparatus change from man to horse power as great smoke-belching engines pulled by spanking trios of chargers replaced the "Wreath of Roses" boys and the "Fly-By-Night" runners.

In the early 1890s, the Firemen's Association of the State of New York announced it would construct a home for indigent firemen at Hudson, N.Y., and that funds would be needed for this purpose.

Though not a wealthy man, but still filled with the great love of his fellow firemen that had made him a leader of men, Harry Howard contributed $1,000 to the Home, the first subscription which later led not only to the construction of the only Firemen's Home but eventually the American Museum of Firefighting, where firemen could get the best of medical care. Chief Howard was present on October 4, 1894, for the dedication of the Home and was given a standing ovation by those present. This is the last written account of the chief to be found in the annals of the Firemen's Home in Hudson.

It is believed that he is buried in the firemen's plot in New York's Greenwood Cemetery. But the city has enshrined his memory forever at a tiny intersection of Canal, Walker, Baxter, and Newberry Streets in lower Manhattan, which is known today as Harry Howard Square. At the Firemen's Museum in Hudson are many mementos of Harry Howard's career, including his helmet, trumpet and two portraits. At the bottom of one portrait these words briefly but capably sum up his career—"He enlisted in a calling which he splendidly arrayed with honors."

A Star Is Born
Barbra Streisand first stepped before footlights leading a goat on Malden Bridge Playhouse set

It was in May of 1957 that a company of 27 young actors and actresses, the largest in the history of the Malden Bridge Playhouse, began arriving in the Columbia County hamlet of Malden Bridge for the summer season ahead. Some of those returning to the Playhouse were familiar names to theater audiences form prior appearances. Stanley Beck, who had won "the most popular actor" award in the summer of 1956 was back, along with Paul Bressoud, producer-manager, and John Hale, who returned to the boards after appearing on a number of television productions during the winter months.

One of the alumni, however, wasn't returning. Audiences the previous year had enjoyed a witty young actor who possessed good timing with his lines and nasal voice. Shelly Berman had written Paul Bressoud he had a single stand-up comic routine at a Catskill Mountain resort. Berman made a good decision: It led him to stardom.

With the entourage of eager young thespians, most of whom came up by train to Chatham from New York, was a small covey of apprentices whose names meant nothing to Playhouse audiences. Their names appeared in small print on the bottom of the playbill. They swept out the theater and frequently helped to make and serve the rather flimsy fare served at "The Lodge," an ancient, rambling structure adjacent to the theater. Once a plant where the famed Hoes hand pumps were manufactured, it served as the "kids" dining and lodging facility.

One of the apprentices was Ingrid Meighan, niece of the noted actor Thomas Meighan and daughter of Mrs. Robert Coates, who at that time resided in Old Chatham. Sharing a small cubicle in "The Lodge" with Ingrid was a slender, young girl making her first trip into the country from her native Brooklyn. Her name appeared in very small print on the program as "Barbara Streisand."

The Playhouse program that summer was an ambitious one opening with "Holiday for Lovers" on June 18. While the actors studied their lines and ran through rehearsals, the apprentices continued their chores, cleaning toilets, painting backdrops and seeking myriad stage properties for forthcoming shows. To Meighan and Barbara Streisand came one pleasant task; they escaped the humdrum work of their fellow neophytes by going to the *Chatham Courier* offices with a program copy and returning the next day to read the proofs.

"I'll never forget that spindly legged kid with the long nose and a pair of almond eyes that seemed to reflect a thousand different thoughts," recalled Frank B. Dayton who was the *Courier's* shop foreman.

Then came the first break for the aspiring young apprentices when the playhouse staged "The Teahouse of the August Moon." Miss Meighan was cast as an Old Woman and the funny looking girl from Brooklyn made her first appearance on the legitimate stage—with no lines, simply leading a goat in front of the footlights.

Barbara (she hated her first name and took the "a" out of it to shape it up after leaving Malden Bridge) tells interviewers, "I don't care what you say about me, just be sure to spell my name wrong." Born in Brooklyn in 1942, she lived a rather depressing life after her father died when she was a year old. A good student, she spent almost all of her hours away from the classroom preparing to be an actress. She never sought roles in school plays. "Why go out for amateurish productions when you can get a role in the real thing," she told her friends.

During the summer of 1956 she worked in a Chinese restaurant to save enough money to get a chance to appear in summer theater. In January of 1957, the Malden Bridge Playhouse inserted a small ad in the *New York Times* that it would hold auditions in New York City. Barbra Streisand took the afternoon off, rode the subway to Manhattan and told John Hale, who interviewed her, that she had enough money to pay her board and be an apprentice. Anyone who had ready cash was welcome, and Barbra returned to Brooklyn to get a gas station map to find a "rinky-dink place called Maaaaalden Bridge by the natives and Mawwwwwlden Bridge by out-of-towners."

Ingrid Meighan, now Mrs. Rene Waldron of Westport, Massachusetts, remembers her roommate as "a very quiet person, almost afraid, who gave me the impression she was trying to cover up her actual age by telling us she was 17." Actually, Streisand had just turned 15 when she made her Malden Bridge debut.

"She had a wonderful sense of humor and was more of a comic than a serious actress," Mrs. Waldron remembers, and her first speaking lines were in a comedy, "The Desk Set," cast as a young secretary to a New York financial tycoon. Her pure Brooklynese accent was as natural as four ninth-inning Dodger errors in the summer of '57. A *Chatham Courier* review of "Desk Set," after giving credit to the major characters, did single out one supporting player. "The Playhouse has a fine young comedienne in Barbara Streisand who makes the most of a vignette role as the office vamp. We hope Mr. Bressoud gives her more of an opportunity in future productions."

The critic's praise seemingly fell on deaf ears, for Barbra Streisand didn't get another speaking role until the weekend after Labor Day in September, when the apprentices staged William Inge's "Picnic."

Unfortunately, there were no reviews on this particular production, presented in matinee performances on the theater lawn.

"Barbra was outstanding as the younger sister," Mrs. Waldron recollects, "and she, by that time, had watched enough performances to absorb a great deal of stage presence."

Another thing that stands out in her memory is the Streisand appetite. "At the Lodge all of us would line up cafeteria style and Barbra was always edging to the front in hopes the food wouldn't give out before she was served. Also, on some of our trips to Chatham, she would stop in at the Boston Candy Kitchen and consume three of Nick Demos' chocolate sodas with vanilla ice cream, at one sitting."

Today, Barbra still has a penchant for food and, according to *Time* magazine, she "neither drinks nor smokes but eats like a woman thrice her weight which is 125 pounds."

In the intervening years, she has won everything: the Emmy for TV, the Grammy for records, the Tony for Broadway and the Oscar for movies. The late Peggy Wood, founder of the Malden Bridge Playhouse, who directed Barbra's stage appearances in 1957, once recalled, "I draw a complete blank on her ability as an actress—but I'll never forget her face."

Bring Back "Chappie" to The Crandell

When the Columbia County Film Festival is held later this year, wouldn't it be fitting to screen one of the movies starring Marguerite Chapman, the Chatham girl who made it good in Hollywood? For those who may not remember her, let's turn back the pages of time and review the career of this talented actress.

The Chapman family lived next door to St. James Church on Hudson Ave. The house is no longer standing and is now the site of the church parking lot. Marguerite's father was an engineer on the Harlem Division Railroad and she was the only girl among four brothers. "Chappie," as she was known at Chatham High, used her height (5' 10") to jump center on the girl's basketball squad.

Graduating in 1936, the family moved to White Plains after Mr. Chapman was transferred by the railroad. Marguerite found employment as a telephone operator where she was taught to modulate her voice and enunciate each word clearly. She then headed for New York City where her lithe, willowy figure, cerulean blue eyes and reddish brown hair attracted the attention of the John Robert Powers Agency, at one time one of the top model agencies in the world. She was soon earning $300 a week appearing on the covers of *Vogue, Harper's Bazaar* and *Vanity Fair.*

At this point, Howard Hughes was looking for a leading lady for *The Outlaw,* and Marguerite was asked to do a screen test. Her work appealed to Hughes and he put the young woman under exclusive contract. Arriving in Hollywood in December 1939, she tested for *The Outlaw* but eventually lost the role to the much ballyhooed screen debut of Jane Russell. Hughes later told Miss Chapman, "You're too much of a lady for the part."

During her acting career, which spanned 20 years, Chapman appeared in nine comedies, four war movies, four mysteries, three crime movies, three westerns, three action films, two science fiction movies, two dramas, two adventures, one musical and one thriller. She did some of her best work in 1942 when she landed at Columbia, a studio which concentrated on profitable war films with an occasional blockbuster thrown in from time to time.

She made five films almost consecutively, including *The Daring Young Man* with Joe E. Brown, *Appointment in Paris* with George

Sanders, *Destroyer* with Edward G. Robinson, *Murder in Times Square* with Edmund Love and *My Kingdom for a Cook* with Charles Coburn.

Destroyer is generally considered her breakout film and she toured the country to promote it. Geared exclusively toward the war effort, she delighted in telling shipyard workers she was there paying tribute to her four brothers in uniform, three in the navy, one in the army.

While under contract to Columbia, Marguerite performed in numerous radio broadcasts on Lux Radio Theatre, Frigidaire Theatre, and Armed Forces Radio with Cary Grant, Herbert Marshall, Dick Powell, Fred MacMurray and Red Skelton. She made only one film in 1944, *Strange Affair,* a comic thriller, but bounded back in 1945 with two excellent efforts, *Counter-Attack* with Paul Muni and *Pardon My Past* with Fred MacMurray.

Miss Chapman finished up her contract at Columbia with *The Walls Came Tumbling Down* with Lee Bowman, *Relentless* with Robert Young, *Coroner's Creek* with Randolph Scott and *The Gallant Blade* with Larry Parks.

Of these, *Relentless* is particularly entertaining. Filmed largely on location near Tucson, Arizona, the picture takes a familiar theme (wronged cowboy becomes an outlaw to clear his name of a murder charge) and adds new polish to it.

As a freelancer, Marguerite worked at RKO in *The Green Promise* (1949) with Walter Brennan and another western, *Kansas Raiders* (1950), at Universal with Audie Murphy portraying legendary badman Jesse James. In 1952, Miss Chapman co-starred with Mitzi Gaynor and Scott Brady in a Runyonesque musical comedy film, *Bloodhounds of Broadway,* and in 1955 she played her last big role in *The Seven Year Itch,* starring Marilyn Monroe.

Miss Chapman then began a lucrative television career and was seen in the *Ford Theatre,* the *Eve Arden Show, Studio One,* the *Ann*

Sothern Show, Perry Mason, Laramie, Marcus Welby, Hawaii Five-O and *Police Story*.

Once relegated to roles which required she only be stoic or sultry, Marguerite over time developed into a fine performer, capable of a wide range of emotions and points of view. Yet, strangely, the better the actress got at her craft, the less she seemed to work. Most fans probably saw her last in 1977 in an installment of *Barnaby Jones*.

Twice divorced, Miss Chapman never had any children but devoted her energies to organizations aiding destitute youngsters. Throughout her lifetime, Marguerite held Chatham close to her heart. She always welcomed Chathamites who visited Hollywood, particularly servicemen and women during World War II.

She corresponded frequently with Chatham friends, among them Russell Northup, who recalls he received a long letter full of recollections after he sent her a photo of the restored Union Station. In the lobby of the Crandell Theatre is an autographed photo sent to the theatre owner Anthony Quirino. It is inscribed "Anthony, my very best to you and my love to Chatham."

Marguerite died in September 1999 at the age of 81. She had often expressed the desire to be interred in Chatham but her remains rest in California.

So, when this year's Film Festival is staged wouldn't it be proper to bring "Chappie" back to the Crandell where, like the rest of us, she enjoyed a balcony seat at 25 cents, and, in her case, perhaps envisioned herself one day on THAT silver screen.

—⇒·◦·⇐—

Chatham . . . Hollywood of the East

As we enter the waning years of the 20th century, Columbia County has become quite blasé when camera crews suddenly appear in our midst and eventually one of our farms, or colleges, or schools becomes the backdrop for a nationally televised film production. The National Broadcasting Company's *GO-USA!* series frequently filmed sequences and entire story plots here, while on rarer occasions, film producers, including Chatham's Harry Belafonte have used a county backdrop to do a full-length film feature.

In 1959, the City of Hudson shivered with delight when Mr. Belafonte, along with the late Robert Ryan and Ed Begley, arrived in the county to do a film version of William McGivern's book, *Odds Against Tomorrow.* Harbel Productions rolled its cameras up and down Warren Street for a bank robbery sequence and, with the magic touch that only Hollywood can bestow, suddenly everyone in Hudson wanted to get into the act. Ham, in its pure and simplest form, was Hudson's bill of fare during that glorious summer of 25 years ago.

From a vantage point 17 miles away, the village of Chatham gave this unusual activity the cold and studied glance of a veteran thespian, because hadn't Chatham been the "Hollywood of the East," when Hudson's closest association with the cinema was a two-day, two-reeler Ben Turpin comedy at The Playhouse on Warren Street. Chatham had undergone the stage-struck pangs 39 years before when the Sphere Motion Picture Corp. moved into town with a hungry-looking young unknown named Norma Shearer to film an opus of the Old West, *By Man's Law.*

Turn the tables back 64 years and see Chatham as it became instantly and madly screen-struck. Mothers left their children to become ladies of questionable virtue in barroom scenes, newspaper men abandoned their desks and typewriters, attorneys gave up their practice of law, ministers left their pulpits and anyone who as much as carried a spear in a Sunday School tableau answered the call of the SILVER SCREEN!

It all began on March 9, 1920, according to *Chatham Courier* files, when there arrived in Chatham a rotund, loquacious gentleman who introduced himself as John S. Lopez and his business card identified him as "Director, Sphere Motion Picture Co., New York City." Mr. Lopez immediately disrupted the normally dull atmosphere of the community when he had printed placards with this clarion call:

COME AND GET INTO PICTURES!

"See yourself in the movies when the picture has its first presentation on the screen at Cady Hall, Chatham. Who knows but there is a Pickford or Chaplin right here among you who needs only the opportunity?"

Chatham, which had known little excitement except for the daily arrival of the Rutland milk train, an occasional illegitimate birth, and the county fair in September, reacted with boundless enthusiasm. Cavernous Cady Hall on Main Street was filled to almost overflowing as Director Lopez began auditioning talent for the film. Two days later he announced he was ready to name the cast which would support Sphere's resident company. Many a stage-struck Chatham girl went to bed that night light of head, nauseous of stomach and short of breath with excitement, but calm enough to offer prayers that she be tapped for a role.

The morning of March 17, 1920, Chatham went completely berserk. The night before, Lem Austin of Chatham, a giant of a man and a conductor on the Harlem Division, had been approached in Grand Central station by a representative of Sphere Motion Picture Co. who asked him if there were any PRIVATE CARS on the Harlem. When Conductor Austin asked why the need for privacy, he was told that "a number of moving picture stars will be taking your train to Chatham."

It didn't take long for Lem Austin to spread the word on his return trip and when the evening train from New York arrived on March 17, there was a large and anxious crowd of awe-struck Chathamites awaiting the arrival of the "movie people" from New York. Mr. Lopez was there and, as if receiving the royal family, made a courtly bow as he helped Lois Lee, a willowy brunette and a favorite of Vitagraph Productions, from the train steps.

To his new Chatham friends, he whispered asides identifying the other members of the cast. There was Harold Forshey, attired in a floppy fedora and cape. "He was the leading man in Elise Janis' last big one," Mr. Lopez hissed. Mr. Forshey flashed a handsome profile and asked the director for the nearest bar. Someone headed him to the Chatham House.

Chatham girls squealed with delight when jaunty William "Bud" Williams, a former champion lightweight boxer who had emerged from the squared circle with an unmarked face, popped through the train doors. "He looks like a Van Heusen shirt ad," sighed a girl and surely he did, high collared, thin of tie, hair parted in the middle, a checked jacket clinging to his powerful shoulders and a flask in his hip pocket.

By this time other passengers, basking in the reflected glory of having ridden from Botanical Gardens through Dover Plains, Philmont and Ghent with "honest-to-God movie stars," fairly vaulted from the train to run home with the news. One even had Harold Forshey's autograph on that day's issue of the *New York*

Sun. Among the last off the train was a spindly girl, who had come with her mother. The kid's name was Norma Shearer. She was what Chathamites would call the "ingin-new."

The next morning Mr. Lopez gathered the cast at Cady Hall and handed out the scripts.

The story line of *By Man's Law* concerned a mountain boy convicted of a murder by circumstantial evidence, who seemed certain to hang from the highest tree unless justice prevailed. Austerlitz was chosen as the site of the hanging.

The Sphere Company had come to Chatham at the suggestion of Mrs. Floyd Buckley, daughter-in-law of Mr. and Mrs. Thomas Buckley, the progenitors of "Buckleyville." A handsome woman, Mrs. Buckley had appeared in several films under her stage name, Lillian Ward. No newcomer to these parts, she had appeared at the Chatham Fair as a talented bareback rider and her equestrian abilities won her a role in the film.

In the script Mrs. Buckley was to discover new evidence to save the condemned mountain boy. Believing it will stay his execution scheduled by the governor for midnight, she starts for the railroad station with the governor's mansion her goal. To her distress she finds the evening train has departed. Undismayed, she leaps into the saddle of a snorting stallion which inexplicably but fortunately is tied near the station. There follows a hell-for-leather ride to the capital, a minute-to-minute confrontation with the governor. He reads the new evidence, orders the hanging postponed, directs a new trial, the mountain boy goes free—justice triumphs!

Miss Mary Eberle of Chatham, an outstanding actress and truly one of America's stage favorites, happened to be "at liberty" at the moment. To her went the coveted role of the boy's mother. John C. Dardess, a handsome Grecian-profiled Chatham attorney, would play Dr. Walter C. Hill, the ingenue's father. Guy M. Hoes of

Chatham, who looked every inch the role, was cast as the governor. His daughter, Adele Hoes Lee, who had just returned from France where she had entertained "our boys" serving overseas, was given the role of Mrs. Hill. More minor roles went to Editor Harry Doty of the *Courier*, Prof. J. Richard Walton, Chatham's master of terpsichore, Frank Massoit, Edward Kline and Thomas S. Buckley. Mr. Doty was cast as the family lawyer, the others "natives" on the stoop of a country store.

Cast rehearsals were held daily at Cady Hall and Mr. Lopez announced the hold-up scene, a key segment of the film, would be shot the following morning. All business halted on Main Street for C. E. Covey's Harness Shop (where Dick and George's Gas Station stands today) had been selected as the backdrop for the nefarious deed. Cameramen cranked, Director Lopez shouted through a megaphone from a second-story window, horsemen thundered in from every direction, women screamed and swooned, guns roared, actors gestured, grimaced, sustained "gut-wounds," fell clutching their abdomens, then straightened out stiffer than stakes. O, glorious day! Nothing had transpired like this since the great fire of '69 had consumed the south half of Main Street!

In his columns Editor Doty, his typewriter touched by a heady feeling of stardom, wrote knowingly, "Chathamites are disconcerted by the bright lights used in the interior scenes. Two arc lamps in front of powerful reflectors are used for this purpose and their brilliance is dazzling."

Dazzled or not, Chathamites cavorted in a series of scenes that saw them prance through filming of a country square dance at the old Klaxton building (later to become a meeting place for the Ku Klux Klan and currently the location of the MacHaydn Theater), enact a quilting bee at Woodman's Hall on School Street and take part in outdoor sequences filmed at Arnold's Mills, Ghent, Malden

Bridge and Buckleyville. The Malden Bridge scene became a disaster when a small herd of grunting pigs invaded and completely wiped out one of Miss Shearer's most dramatic effects.

After shooting 50,000 feet of celluloid which Director Lopez said would be reduced to 5,800 on the screen, the stars, extras and almost everyone else in Chatham joined in a community party on the spacious lawns of the Louis F. Payn residence to celebrate completion of the film. "An excellent collation it was and an ample supply of ice cream was provided by the Sphere Company," wrote Editor Doty, who finally left the glare of the arc lights and got back to his writing tasks.

Of the stars little is known, except the late Norma Shearer, who went on to become one of the nation's favorite screen idols. Floyd Buckley, who had the brief role of the frustrated hangman, later devoted his entire life to the stage, radio and television. At the time of his death in August 1958, he had a lead role in the stage production of "No Time for Sergeants" on Broadway.

The majority of those who took part in *By Man's Law* have gone to the great movie house in the sky and strangely, Editor Doty failed to recall the reception of the film when it premiered at Cady Hall. One can only presume that it bombed on Main Street.

A few of those who appeared before the cameras are still with us and revel in the memories when they were touched by the hand of Thespis and got their jollies in the throes of cinematic hysteria during the summer of 1920 when Chatham was "the Hollywood of the East."

———❖———

Good Old Nostalgia Run Amok

As we old codgers become more ancient each day, nostalgia runs amok. With ever increasing violence in films and television and expletives punctuating every new book, Ira Gershwin was right when he penned "Authors, who once knew better words now only use four letter words writing prose." How true! "Anything Goes!" As family values disappear, I long for the days when mom, dad and the kids were family and did things together and enjoyed doing them. Are you old enough to remember when it was an event to ride out into the countryside together, going no place in particular but singing together all the way. So was a Sunday outing to a favorite restaurant, Rainbow's End in Valatie, Keeler's in Albany or the Red Lion Inn in Stockbridge.

Whatever happened to Lucky Strike Green? It went to war after Pearl Harbor and never came back. A casualty? Missing in action? In our family, we read books together. On winter evenings my father would read to me and my boyhood friends. Kipling, Arthur Conan Doyle, James Fenimore Cooper were nightly favorites. I recall I had a rather large library by the time I was 12 and frequently read aloud with my mother correcting my pronunciation. I don't believe families do much reading together anymore. Reading inability in schools is as common today as our Everhard #2 pencils.

But I don't mean to imply that ours was a sticky-sweet-togetherness-family. We did things together, but we also had our private pleasures which seem quite simplistic in today's world. There was no television in the 1930s, so we gathered around the radio to hear "The FBI In Action," broadcast by WGY, or Ed Wynn, "The Texaco Fire

Chief" on WEAF, New York. In the morning we listened to Charles John Stevenson ("The Chanticleer") and Kinderhook's Ed Mitchell's "Farm Program of the Air" also on WGY. I, on the other hand, late every afternoon had the radio all to myself for "The Shadow," "Little Orphan Annie," and "I raised the Flag for Hudson High" and "Jack Armstrong, the All-American Boy."

Today, rap singers spew filth, but in yesteryears there was no swearing or you got your mouth washed out with soap and sent to your room. That's what happened when my second-grade teacher told my mother I had called Arthur Danyew an "SOB." It was a time when adults used substitutes for swear words especially in front of the children. "Dang it!" "Gosh darn!" or "Gol darn it!"

I only heard my father swear once on the night the Chatham Shirt Factory burned on Church Street. That meant a large number of men and women would be out of work. Father always dressed properly, even in the middle of the night to cover a story for the *Courier*. As he put on his hat the word "damn!" escaped from his lips.

Whatever happened to glass milk bottles? John Blinn, who lived on lower Payn Avenue, delivered our milk. He came before dawn, but just before sun-up we would go out on the back porch and find two bottles of milk, the kind with a bulging bubble on top. Cream in the milk rose naturally into the bubble and could be poured off by capping the bubble with a curved spoon as a stopper. Voila! You had rich cream for coffee and a bottle of skimmed milk for dieters. Do you remember on frigid mornings when the cream would pop right out of the bottle but would recede back when brought into a warm kitchen?

Whatever happened to running boards? They were fun to ride on with the wind blowing our hair (when we had hair) and billowing our shirts, feeling for all the world like policemen on a chase. What ever happened to tea dancing? What ever happened to Lester Lenin's music and the little caps he passed out to dancers. When it was upbeat you could do the Shag or Lindy Hop or if it was slower you could try the Princeton Dip. I didn't have much luck with the Dip, as my high school love, Helen Underwood, had bad knees and she'd end up on the floor each time we did the required bending of the bodies.

And then there were Sunday dinners at home immediately after church services. From time to time, the rector and his wife would be invited. Always an important event, the main course was usually roast beef (prime ribs were 49 cents a pound in 1932). Dessert was a chocolate cake with fudge frosting baked the day before, because it was the good clergyman's favorite, accompanied by home-made vanilla ice cream. We all sat at the big dining room table—all together, never a smaller table for the children—and we were expected to use our best manners and our best behavior. No elbows on the table, no talking with food in your mouth and never speak while adults are having a conversation. Believe me, we were on our best behavior and enjoyed it, being accepted as almost equals by the grownups.

One of the great theatrical productions some 40 years ago was the annual Tri-Village Fire Co. Minstrel Show staged in the Old Chatham Grange Hall to SRO audiences. A highlight was the banter between the end men, written by Larry Gelbart. I played "Sassafras" and the late Peter Townsend next to me was "Molasses." We drew the biggest yaks taking corny cracks at our home towns. For example:

"Chatham is a small town? The all-night restaurant closes at 4:30 P.M."

"Just before the wedding, the best man took the groom aside and said, 'You don't want to marry that girl, everybody in Ghent has had her.' So the groom said, 'Is Ghent such a big place?'"

"East Chatham is so backward the yogurt doesn't have any culture."

"Most towns have public restrooms. Old Chatham has a pay bush."

"Did you hear all the garbage collections in North Chatham have been canceled. The goat died."

"How dull is Valatie? If it wasn't for mouth-to-mouth resuscitation, there wouldn't be any romance at all."

"How small is Malden Bridge? The zip code is a fraction!"

They don't stage shows like that any more. Now I can see why.

——>·<——

Manhattan Is Still a Helluva Town

A year ago this week on 9/11, the nation's second "day of infamy," terrorists struck Gotham but failed to terrorize New Yorkers, and the Big Apple, with a big chunk out of it, is still a pippin. Noo-Yawk-Noo-Yawk may have been broke, battered and bewildered, but it has rebounded and still ranks as the greatest city in the world.

What is Gotham? It's a chauffeured limo at the curb, frequent garbage bags on the sidewalk, and a million-dollar necklace in Van Cleef's window. Most of its future is in the past. And what a past— but the power and the glory live on in the penthouses, in the corridors of executive suites, the best restaurants. In New York, every day may be mugger's day and every night a screech of sirens, but this is and always will be a reigning metropolis.

I have been in love with the city since the day as a small boy I stepped off the Chatham train at Grand Central. It was Christmastime and a chorale of Red Caps sent Christmas carols echoing through the vast terminal and also sent shivers down my spine. There are so many things I like about New York. The startlingly clean city buses. The sprawling, fairy-land of lighted trees outside the Tavern on the Green, the Plaza Hotel with its timeless paneled walls and wing-collared waiters (or at least the last time I dined in the departed Oak Room),

New York Newsday, most readable of the city's dailies despite a plethora of ugly ads. The nightly theater rush when, in a trice, the city's 12,000 honking cabs suddenly disappear and the streets fall silent.

The great lions outside the public library (jokes about reading between the lions are inadmissible), and let's not forget that the Tilden family of New Lebanon set up the trust to establish the library.

The endless expanse of the Metropolitan Museum, the Staten Island ferry terminal, the seedy office buildings on Seventh Avenue that house every clothing designer you ever heard of, from Ralph Lauren to Pauline Trigère. Michael's Pub on E. 55th where Woody Allen indeed sits in for a set each Monday evening with the house band. What kind of clarinetist is Woody? Well, he shouldn't give up his daytime job.

Let's go back to those city buses for a moment. They carry six million passengers a day, and each bus looks as though it had been scrubbed and polished that very morning, which may be the case. Being slightly obsessed, I have looked at passing buses all over the island; I have peered inside at every opportunity, and I am impressed. People-watching, the best outdoor sport in Manhattan. There goes Kitty Carlisle Hart, a 92-year-old filly, and here comes Peter Duchin (tieless, blazered). Pop into a cocktail party and there's Peter Jennings, Betty Friedan, Mike Wallace, Peter Maas, and Tom Wolfe. This isn't namedropping; they are neighbors living around the corner and borrowing a cup of royalties from one another.

"But you wouldn't want to LIVE there," is the out-of-towner's Manhattan mantra. Maybe not year-round, but I toyed with the idea in the years immediately following World War II. The city was at its glamorous peak and the repository of the best of everything. The Stork Club and El Morocco, the Copa and the Latin Quarter, "21," the Colony Club and Henri Soulé's Pavilion, a restaurant that would never be equaled.

Everybody who was anybody seemed to live just around the corner from one another in the great apartments and town houses on the Upper East Side. Today, New York is a brave city. Nobody wails or weeps over the tremendous changes that have sorely damaged the most exciting city in the world, but maybe the subject is still too painful to discuss.

Manhattan, a great drink with a cherry in it; a classic Rodgers and Hart song with a lilt to it; a long and skinny island abuzz and alive. It has been bum-rapped to death but it refuses to die. Not only did it withstand the 9/11 tragedy, but it is overcoming problems with crime, pollution, and corruption. Let's give Rudy the cheers (loudly) for that.

The cops and firemen are smartly uniformed, look wise and move slowly, except when they are called to place their lives on the line. Blessed heroes, every man jack of them.

New York, New York, yeah, the town so big they named it twice. The Great White Way has been cleansed until it shines 99.9 percent pure just like Ivory soap, and at this writing, there are 50 live plays and musicals going at the moment. By-the-by, don't worry, the Rockettes will still be kicking when Santa comes to town.

It's not altogether true that "if you make it there"—here—"you'll make it anywhere" but this is still where everybody wants to make it, if only to be able to escape. Sadly, there is no longer a Walter Winchell to sing Manhattan's praises—in fact the old Broadway columnist has long gone to that Fourth Estate in the sky—and this great newspaper town is down to a handful of dailies, but there is no moaning at the bar; New Yorkers live for the moment.

New Yorkers are oxymoronic to the max; funny-sad; tough-sweet; angry-resigned. It's a fascinating mix, also to the max. God bless 'em, every one.

CELEBRATIONS

The Case of the Missing Apostrophe

Halloween. It's here and it's a case for the apostrophe posse. The Case of the Missing Apostrophe. When I was a nipper it was Hallowe'en. The apostrophe was for a missing "v" for this holiday from hell, which began with a celebration known as All Hallow's Day, better known as All Saints Day. Yes, a strange and exotic observance for us American squares, so dark, so Gothic, so Middle Ages. Witches with warts on their tongues, yowling black cats with arched backs, muffled screams at midnight. Oh, and pumpkins. I don't know what pumpkins have to do with it, but they are grinning away like Big Bad Bill caught with Paula Jones.

Halloween was pretty tame stuff when I was a kid growing up on Payn Avenue in Chatham. We were simply unimaginative or unimaginably simple. An old bed sheet served as a costume. We didn't have fancy masks but just darkened our faces with smudges of burnt cork. The only prank we could think to play consisted of soaping windows. "Trick or Treat" hadn't been invented yet, nor had UNICEF, which I guess was responsible for the practice. The treat is usually candy, which is bad for kid's teeth, so the trick is on them. Dentists living along the routes tend to hand out toothbrushes and toothpaste samples and are to be eschewed. After eschewing, "Spit!" as dentists are so fond of ordering.

We like to recall the Halloween night when our neighbor, Frank Abriel, vowed that "those rascals won't tip over our outhouse this year, by gum." Shortly after dark, he grabbed his double-barreled shotgun and loaded it. One cartridge contained rock salt, the other bird shot. In previous years, the rascals has always pushed the privy over from the door side. So he left the door open a crack with the muzzle of the gun sticking out. A gust of wind blew up through the hole next to him, rattling the loose pages of the mail order catalogue hanging on the wall. There was a rattling sound on the roof. He sprang into action, both ear and gun cocked. Only a branch rubbing the roof in the freshening October night's wind.

Suddenly, the little house started to shake and groan. But the rascals were attacking from the back, instead of the door side as he had anticipated they would. When the family heard him screeching for help, they rushed to the scene only to find him on his back bravely firing through one of the outhouse holes and then the other, barely missing George (Hotstuff) Coffin's huge white gelding that by day pulled Mr. Coffin's coal wagon. The horse ran and whinnied about the night pasture to the delight of the rascals hiding nearby. Mr. Abriel never found his upper plate.

Strong-armed farm boys loved Halloween. Heavy four-wheeled farm wagons would be seen the next morning astride the roof of the local livery stable. One morning the good residents of Philmont were startled to see an enormous sign that had in some mysterious way been placed on a tall smoke stack of the Harder Mills. Special rigging equipment had to be ordered from Albany to get it down. For days after one Halloween, the residents of Hillsdale were mystified because the church bell would ring out in the night waking the good residents from their slumber. Armed with a lantern and shotgun, the sexton would sneak up into the belfry, but no one was there!

Ingenious lads they were! More than 300 feet of clothesline had been tied to the bell clapper and then let out through a louver in the side of the belfry and into a pasture lot. After three nights of disturbed sleep, some were predicting dire happenings. There was nervous tension and the good people of Hillsdale were whispering. Why would the bell's clanging echo through the Taconic hills at three in the morning? At last the sexton discovered the clothesline during a daylight search of the belfry, restoring peace and quiet to the natives. In Valatie, a newly painted lumber box wagon was a tempting object. It was tipped over during the night. Pinned under it, they found a town constable who had been lying in it for hours waiting to catch the pranksters. In those days brawn was more important then jelly beans.

Halloween is no longer small-town or small time. Like Christmas, it has turned into a season. Otherwise perfectly normal people plan their Halloween activities weeks in advance. Costumes get ever more elaborate. Stores have "Halloween Sales" with scary prices. Halloween has, by some estimates, become a $1.5 million-a-year business, not including candy sales.

I don't want to be a party pooper, even if I am. I admire the trouble people go to for what they assume is a good time. Besides, I have the kind of face that doesn't require a mask. All I have to do is put on my glasses and some mean dame is sure to ask, "When you take off your glasses does the nose go with them?" What am I going to do this Halloween? I'm putting out my usual empty candy jar with the sign "Take One" and going to bed early.

Reflections on Dec. 5: Happy Birthday, Martin!

By this time, it seems that everyone should recall that December 5 is Martin Van Buren's birthday. It is also Saint Nicholas' Eve, a children's holiday traditionally kept by the Dutch.

Van Buren was born in 1782. President Van Buren never left word of what it was like to have a birthday on Saint Nicholas' eve. But traditions handed down suggest that custom surrounding the day lingered on for many years.

At some unknown point in time, Saint Nicholas' Eve ceased to be observed in America. Its customs, however, were kept alive. "On the Night Before Christmas" and a New Yorker, Clement Clark Moore, virtually created an American tradition when Moore published his famous poem in the *Troy Sentinel* in 1823. Legend has it, that Moore penned his now famous poesy while visiting friends in Claverack. Saint Nicholas' sleigh is a thoroughly New York Dutch addition, yet it is impossible to account for the reindeer. Two of them, "Donner" and "Blitzen" (Thunder and Lightning), have Dutch names.

To judge from the size of the chimney that Saint Nicholas slid down, the house was most assuredly a Dutch one—but probably renovated, for the poem's narrator speaks of throwing open first the shutters and then the sash. Interior shutters and sash windows were changes made to Dutch homes in the late 18th century. And by the chimney, carefully hung stockings replaced wooden ones.

Our eighth president was known to be a man of great taste in clothes and his creature comforts, particularly wine and food. Michael Henderson, a former curator at Lindenwald, was asked to list some of Van Buren's favorite comestibles.

"In looking for this information," Henderson said, "I found myself glimpsing a world of epicurean delights which reflects not only upon Van Buren as a gastronome, but also upon the public perception of him in the 19th century as being extravagant. Van Buren received harsh criticism during his political career for being a bon vivant. Expensively and handsomely dressed and formal in his manners, the Whig Party often exaggerated these qualities of Van Buren for their own personal gains."

One of the most famous cartoons of the infamously dirty campaign of 1840, which Van Buren lost, pictured his rival William Henry Harrison drinking a mug of good ol' hard cider, while Van Buren daintily sipped a glass of vintage White House Champagne. During Van Buren's term in the White House, his colleagues recalled attending many "charming little dinners."

In a famous attack against the excesses of the Van Buren administration, Pennsylvania Congressman Charles Ogle blustered on for several days criticizing the president's spending and mentioning Van Buren's penchant for "fricandeau de veau and omelettes soufflés" as well as expensive tableware.

When Van Buren purchased Lindenwald, he renovated the 43-year-old house with a large banquet hall featuring a Duncan Phyfe accordion-style extension dining table which seated over 20 guests. In later years, the table passed into other hands but through the efforts of the Friends of Lindenwald, the table is on loan from its present owners and graces the entrance hall. Lindenwald was always well stocked with an abundant larder including a large wine cellar with the finest Madeira and Champagne. The household staff always included a cook and a waitress or two.

Van Buren ran Lindenwald as a working farm. Gardens and greenhouses kept the table filled with fresh vegetables in summer as well as potatoes and root vegetables in winter. Turkey, beef, and mutton were frequently served along with fresh fish acquired at Stuyvesant Landing.

A visitor at Lindenwald commented that Van Buren "always began the day with a 10- to 15-mile ride on his horse 'Duroc' often as far as Peter Groat's Tavern in Chatham. This would be followed by a hearty breakfast, then he would engage with workmen until he would tire and then retire to the library which he constantly enlarged."

From the president's youngest son, Smith Thompson Van Buren, we have this description of one of his father's first dinners at Lindenwald: "The dish before him contained a fine ham; then comes two side dishes of potatoes and peas; then an enormous fricassee; then cucumbers, beets, beans and fresh corn and then in front of John another supply of fricassee. Four bottles of champagne completed the carte for the first course. Then second was pies, custard, jelly—of excellent make—and the third of fine-flavored seegars (sic.)"

Hold the bicarb . . .

——◆——

A Holiday's Durable Myths and Realities

"It pleased God to visit us with death dayly, and with so general a disease that the living were scarce able to burie the dead."

Gov. William Bradford, Plymouth, Mass.

Much of their powerful story is shrouded in myth and half truth. They were common folk, not aristocrats and barely able to read or write. Though religious rebels, they were not Puritans—who arrived in America a decade later—but a robust and fun-loving people, mixing their piety with merriment. Next weekend, as elsewhere across the United States, we will celebrate a holiday traditionally regarded as uniquely American, commemorating the first Thanksgiving of the Pilgrims at Plymouth Rock in 1621. The party must have been a rouser; a three-day bash, Indians and all, with feasting, drinking, games, hangovers. Afterward, Gov. William Bradford described some of the participants as "madd bacchanalians" and noted that colony folk were left in a surly mood because the "beer and strong waters had been nearly consumed."

When I was in Eva Wadsworth's fourth grade in Chatham Union School, we had to dress up in Pilgrim costumes, with severe black hats, buckled shoes and white starched collars for a classroom pageant. It was my task to recite the famous poem by Felicia Hemans about the landing at Plymouth Rock, which began, "The breaking waves dashed high on a stern and rock-bound coast and the woods against a stormy sky their giant beaches toss'd . . . " I didn't know then that the seashore at Plymouth was not "stern and rock-bound" at all, but flat and sandy, nor did I know that Mrs. Hemans, a pious and imaginative soul, never actually saw the coast, or America either. She was an English housewife who wrote the poem in 1826 after reading a newspaper account in Ryllon, Wales, of the 1824 celebration of Forefather's Day at Plymouth, Mass. Her poem became enormously popular on both sides of the Atlantic, causing Forefather's Day—until then an obscure New England tradition—to become a national event. Thanksgiving Day was finally proclaimed by President Abraham Lincoln in the 1860s.

And yet to me, Thanksgiving has always symbolized much that is basic in America. Just what is the soul of Thanksgiving? The answer is simple—leftovers. You may think that pumpkin pie for Thanksgiving is the pinnacle of the holiday. But there are plenty of others that think pumpkin pie for breakfast on Friday after giving thanks makes up for all the rest of the year's oatmeal and corn flakes. Just think, if you manage it properly, and have enough pies, you can probably have pie for breakfast for a week. After all, pumpkin pie is only eggs, vegetable, and milk with a little pastry underneath. That's easily a nutritious breakfast.

And apple pie—apples, sugar and pie crust—a great breakfast treat! Save the mince for last, not only because it will keep best, but also because there's something about the sweet-sour taste that is appropriate for a sentimental finale. For many families, the divvying up of the Thanksgiving leftovers will be as much of a production as getting the meal on the table.

The suspense is over—the turkey was juicy as always and the children (and adults) behaved well throughout the meal. This is not the time to argue about naps (for children and adults) or who had the best football team or whether both mashed white and candied sweet potatoes should have been prepared. An hour or two of polite conversation in the living room next Thursday gives the serving dishes time to cool to handling temperatures. It also gives all the dinner-table companions time to reflect on how to divide up the leftovers. The production of leftovers is part of the Thanksgiving meal. There will be a plate with turkey and all the fixings to take to someone who is missing a meal.

Then the serious business of making up family packages begins. The creamed onions are easily divided, as can be the whipped potatoes and squash. There can be serious thought given to the stuffing. Crisp, over-baked stuffing for some. Others prefer the moister in-the-bird version. Some get both, of course. That brings the kitchen crew to the bird. The breakdown crew always seems larger than the pre-meal crew. But that just may be because the tablecloth and silverware contingent come out to make sure their tastes are fully represented in packing the take-home version of dinner.

Dismantling is serious business. The sharp knife cuts through the joints and there is careful attention given to white and dark meat so that each person receives a favored morsel. A wing for a small soup pot and some back meat for a turkey casserole are added to the pile of supper-and-sandwich-sized slices. And at the last minute don't forget to pack some cranberry sauce, some gravy and those extra rolls that always seem to be on hand. Baggies have made the little dishes and containers of my youth all obsolete. Everything can just be apportioned, sealed and put into the larger plastic bags for transport. Leaving someone with the turkey carcass is a foregone conclusion. But that is the ultimate prize in the leftover category. Once stripped of the bite-sized pieces of meat for sandwiches and just good eating, the person who gets the turkey bones can make soup. Real turkey soup, with onions, celery and snips of carrots with barley thrown in, is the leftover to warm the heart on a cold winter night. You don't even have to enjoy the soup immediately. After a week of turkey sandwiches and casserole, you can just put the soup in the freezer, where it will be ready to remind you of the glorious meal and the dear people who joined you for it.

Thanksgiving is an okay holiday. All that business of Pilgrims and Indians sitting down together, breaking bread and each others' heads. Friends to the end—which often came quite suddenly. They probably gnawed on venison short ribs. That cut down on who wanted the white meat, should we serve claret or white Bordeaux—and so on. Families were very nuclear then, with short fuses. Norman Rockwell always painted them before the actual fighting broke out, but if you look closely at a Rockwell painting of a Thanksgiving dinner, you just know there are a few troublemakers there. For instance, some Moral Majority people who'd refuse to eat the Pope's nose.

Thanksgiving was the day in your youth when we played Indian. The day wouldn't have been complete without it. There are plenty of feathers from the turkey. The bird has been strutting around the yard for several months. Two turkeys were fattened each year. One for Thanksgiving, the other for Christmas. The day before Thanksgiving one of the birds went before the firing squad. We kids got the feathers. We shaded our eyes and glanced down the lines of elms that bordered Payn Avenue. "Paleface soldiers coming," we told each other. "Head them off at the pass, ugh." The "ugh" proved you were talking fluent Sioux. On most days, soldiers and cowboys won these battles, but not on Thanksgiving. Keep tuned and I'll have some more on my favorite holiday come Thursday a week.

Magic of Christmas Comes a Day Early

Like so many of the moments in our lives, the reality of Christmas seldom ever lives up to the expectation. I guess that is why I always like Christmas Eve better. Christmas Eve is a day of dreams, a day of squirming anticipation. A fantasy day on which most things seem more beautiful and all things are possible. Shopping is done. Presents are wrapped. Decorations are hung. All that remains is the magic.

My most unforgettable Christmas Eve occurred during World War II, on December 24, 1944, to be exact. General Patton's mighty Third U.S. Army had ground to a halt in eastern France near Metz, its gasoline diverted to British forces in the north at Churchill's request and Roosevelt's. It was a magical night in the village of La Croix-sur-Meuse where we were billeted. During the years of German occupation, the French had been unable to celebrate midnight mass because of a curfew imposed by the Wehrmacht. Any Frenchman wandering the street after dark stood a good chance of being shot.

The stars shone brilliantly and a serene stillness embraced the Lorraine countryside. The fragrance of wood smoke hung heavily in the air. The villagers gathered in the square and we were invited to join the procession to the church. Candles were handed out. Each of us carried one to light our way through the darkened streets of the village whose electricity had not yet been restored following an Allied air raid. Then, from the front of the procession, a few voices were lifted in the ancient hymn, "Minuit Chrétien" and a triumphant chorus responded.

The old church was cold and damp, yet the spirit of Christmas Eve warmed the hearts, the inner being and the voices of those who now could call themselves "Free French."

The priest's homily that Christmas Eve was a message to God for the gift of His son and the American troops who had liberated the village. The Battle of the Bulge was underway to the north in Belgium, and prayers were offered for the men under siege at Bastogne. After the service, we joined in a joyful "reveillon," a post-midnight collation served in the town hall accompanied by toasts to the New Year of 1945 and earnest wishes that the war would come to a successful conclusion 'ere another year passed.

The next morning we located our gear, climbed in our vehicles and headed out. General Patton's Third Army would thunder northward in the next 28 hours to relieve Bastogne, but over the years the serenity of that Christmas Eve spoke Peace on Earth and Good Will Toward Men. It will never be forgotten.

In my parents' home, Christmastime was the day that the tree, which had stood bare and green for a week in the barn, finally came into the house and took its stand in a corner of the library.

Actually, we did not have a Christmas tree when I was very young. My father, a dedicated environmentalist, did not believe in cutting down evergreens, but by the time I was seven or eight, a tree was cut and the redolence of the pine boughs added to the spirit of Christmas that filled the old house. The ritual of decorating the tree became a tradition. It was father's job to weave the strings of lights through the branches.

It was mother's job to arrange the sequined felt skirt around the trunk. It was my job to hang the glass icicles that had been my father's when he was a boy (it was mother's job to rearrange the ornaments and icicles after I had gone to bed). Then came the most magical moment of all. The lamps on the end tables were turned off. The colored lights woven through the tree were turned on. For long silent moments, we sat as a family and basked in the glow of the magic we had created.

The silence, I suspect, is what made it all so special. The radio had been turned off. There was no television to interrupt this blessed interval in our lives. There was peace in our house. Peace and warmth and quiet calm. Sometime during the night, after I had gone to bed, the angel had flown to the top of the tree and presents came out of their hiding places to take their places beneath the branches. I had gone to my room with the firm belief that on Christmas Eve, on such a night, all things were possible, all hopes would be realized.

Wonder of wonders, Santa Claus had not forgotten my wishes and surely the flat box wrapped in green with a white bow just had to be the "cowboy suit" I wanted. I had even written a letter to Santa Claus at station WGY in Schenectady and he had read my name over the air and let everyone know within a 50,000 watt radius that I wanted a "cowboy suit" but carefully did not add that he would bring one in his pack.

The dream of every boy in Eva Wadsworth's fourth grade was to have a pair of high-top boots with a built-in scabbard at the top of one boot to hold a scout knife. The square package wrapped in snowman paper must be my coveted boots that I had seen in the window of the Brown Shoe Company. O' glorious day! The little box covered with shiny gold paper was a mystery, but it had to be something special because everyone knew that good things come in small packages.

The dreams of Christmas Eve almost always give way to disappointment in the bright light of Christmas morning and especially,

Christmas morning of 1929. Chatham, along with the rest of the nation, was still reeling from the stock market crash. The Great Depression had enveloped each and every family. Fathers were out of work and for many children, there would be no presents at all.

The cowboy suit with the pearl-handled six-shooters and a gun-belt full of silver bullets turned out to be a flannel shirt and corduroy knickers. The lace-up leather boots with the knife would end up being a desk lamp. Good things may come in small packages, but so do socks.

Like so many of the moments in our lives, Christmas Day never quite lives up to our dreams. But, then, it is a tough act to follow. But all in all, Christmas is a delightful mish-mash of fables, legends and traditions. In our Hudson Valley, Dutch children put their shoes by the chimney and filled them with hay or a carrot for Saint Nicholas' great white horse. This fine steed flew over rooftops enabling the patron saint of sailors and Dutch trading towns to dispense presents through the chimney, replacing straw or carrot with sweets and trinkets (if they were good) or switches (if they were not).

Few records survive to indicate how long this Dutch custom was kept in the Hudson Valley, but one song preserved among New York Dutch families is "Sancte Claus good heilig man."

> Santa Claus, good holy man.
> Put on your tabard, the best you can,
> Go clad in it to Amsterdam.
> From Amsterdam then go to Spain,
> and there golden apples
> And bright pomegranates
> Roll through the streets.
> Santa Claus, my dear good friend,
> I have always served you;
> If you will now give me something,
> I'll serve you my life long.

And hey, Santa, I may even forgive you for not bringing me that cowboy suit and the leather boots from Brown's.

———⊰◆⊱———

Choose a Patron to Work for You

SAN MIGUEL DE ALLENDE—It is a Mexican custom to celebrate one's saint's day. Every evening, the local television channel lists the names of persons observing their *onomastico*—saint's day. Many families name their children after the saint of the day on which they were born. There is a saint assigned for almost every day of the year, but regardless of the date of your birthday, you celebrate your saint's day.

For example, if your birthday is January 23, you have the traditional party on that date and if your name is Michael or Miguel, you celebrate on San Miguel day and it is said that there are so many churches in San Miguel that you could attend mass in a different church every day of the year. That's not quite true but the various churches do mark their saint's day—San Francisco, San de Dios, San Filipe, etc. There are usually day-long celebrations with band concerts, a parish dinner and, of course, fireworks and dancing into the night.

Saints have been traditionally associated with a disease or disability, an occupation, profession or other activity. Through prayer, people seek their intercession with God for cures, for protection or for the fostering of activity. Their designation as a patron saint usually arose through popular devotion. In some instances, however, the Roman Catholic Church has officially named patron saints.

Accountants: St. Matthew

Actors: St. Genesuis

Artists: St. Bernardino of Siena

Architects: St. Thomas the Apostle, St. Barbara

Athletes: St. Sebastian

Authors: St. Francis de Sales

Aviators: Our Lady of Loreto; St. Terese of Liseux; St. Joseph of Cupertino

Booksellers: St. John of God

Builders: St. Vincent Ferrer

Butchers: St. Anthony of Egypt; St. Hadrian; St. Luke

Carpenters: St. Joseph

Chefs: St. Lawrence; St. Martha

Dentists: St. Apollonia

Editors: St. John Basco

Farmers: St. George; St. Isidore

Firemen: St. Florian

Fishermen: St. Andrew

Hunters: St. Hubert; St. Eustachius

Infantrymen: St. Maurice

Journalists: St. Francis de Sales

Jurists: St. Catherine of Alexandria; St. John of Capistrano

Laborers: St. Isidore; St. James; St. John Basco

Lawyers: St. Ivo; St. Genesius; St. Thomas Moore

Librarians: St. Jerome

Mariners: St. Michael; St. Nicholas of Tolentino

Medical Social Workers: St. John Regis

Medical Technicians: St. Albert the Great

Merchants: St. Francis of Assisi; St. Nicholas of Myra

Musicians: St. Gregory the Great; St. Cecilia; St. Dunstan

Nurses: St. Camellus de Lellis; San Raphael

Painters: St. Luke

Pharmacists: Sts. Cosmas and Damian; St. James the Great

Physicians: St. Pantaleon; Sts. Cosmas and Damian; St. Luke; St. Raphael

Policemen: St. Michael

Postal Workers: St. Gabriel

Priests: St. Jean-Baptiste Vianney

Public Relations Specialists: St. Bernardino of Siena

Radiologists: St. Michael

Sailors: St. Cuthbert; St. Brendan

Scientists: St. Albert

Sculptors: St. Claude

Secretaries: St. Genesius

Singers: St. Gregory; St. Cecil

Social Workers: St. Louise de Marillac

Soldiers: St. George; St. Joan of Arc; St. Ignasius

Stenographers: St. Genesius

Students: St. Thomas Aquinas; St. Catherine of Alexandria

Surgeons: Sts. Cosmas and Damian

Tailors: St. Homobonus

Tax Collectors: St. Matthew

Taxi Drivers: St. Fiacre

Teachers: St. Gregory the Great; St. Catherine of Alexandria

Working men: St. Joseph

Writers: St. Francis de Sales

Brides: St. Nicholas of Myra

Housewives: St. Anne

Mothers: St. Monica

Deaf: St. Francis de Sales

Invalids: St. Roch

Mentally Ill: St. Dympna

Rheumatism: St. James the Greater
Travelers: St. Anthony of Padua

—————

Electric Park
Everyone Packed Up the Children for a Day
at Kinderhook Lake 67 Years Ago

It's June, 10, 1904, and where to spend the weekend? The answer was obvious to Columbia County residents 67 years ago. There was only one place to go for fun and excitement—Electric Park, Kinderhook Lake. The park had been opened in 1901 by the Albany and Hudson Railroad which operated a line of "electric cars," as they were called, between the two cities. The cars were propelled by contact with a third rail which was heavily charged with electricity, a power which frequently brought a speedy end to life to both humans and animals.

Located on the east bank of Kinderhook Lake, the park was built to attract patrons of the railroad and encourage travel over its rails. The family a half century ago found myriad delights amid the towering trees in the park. There were stands where souvenirs, trinkets, gimcracks, and trifles were sold in abundance. Nearby were canoes and boats to sail over Kinderhook's placid waters. Music from the carousel blended with the mighty crankings and clankings of a Ferris wheel and near this point of merrymaking was a high diving tower where several times a day, a gentleman clad in spectacular trunks would plunge 60 feet into the lake waters. He was introduced as "Professor Speedy" and made his dive accompanied by a long roll of drums.

Ponies and goats chewed grass contentedly awaiting the moment when they would be hitched to carts and driven around the park grounds by adult and children alike. The principal attraction, however, was the Rustic Theater. It was built on a slope over the lakeside and bleacher seats for 400 persons sloped toward the stage. Over the seating arrangement was a canopy to guard against inclement weather. For the first two years the railroad offered a company of troubadours who each week presented a different opera.

These musical treats were just too much for the taste of Columbians and in 1903 a vaudeville program was substituted. Later moving pictures were presented as part of the evening performance.

On almost every summer evening hundreds of persons rode the electric cars or came by horse to view this marvelous spot of entertainment. Those who traveled by the trolley were constantly in fear that they might never reach the park or return home. It was a one-track road and cars were supposed to meet at a siding. Unfortunately, this did not always happen and in the early days a bad wreck occurred on the road which cost several lives.

Crossing the lake from the park was a wooden bridge built on piles which led to what was then known as "the point." The span remained for only a short while, and one severe winter the pressure of ice caused it to collapse and visitors had to travel a circuitous route by horse and wagon to reach the area. Here was located the Point Hotel and each year on its grounds during August was held the famous Farmer's Picnic. This event was the biggest social occasion of the season for farm families and they came by the hundreds to enjoy the festivities.

In the light of modern times it would probably not cause a ripple of excitement, but 50 years ago the tempo of life was much slower. To the picnic came country folk for a reunion with those whom they had not seen since the previous August. Luncheons were spread under the trees, and then an hour or so later, an orator would hold forth. As evening approached the men gathered together to discuss what men usually discuss at events of this type—farm products, politics, and the forthcoming Chatham Fair. A pall of blue cigar smoke hung over the gentlemen while, at a safe distance away, the ladies gathered to exchange recipes and to marvel at the growing families whose progeny at this very moment were running and playing on the shores of the lake. As the sun dipped in the west, the family men left the circle capped with smoke, the ladies swept the crumbs from the tablecloths, the children were gathered up and the homeward trip was begun.

But there were those who were anxious to remain and discuss more fully the political notes of the day. The name of President Theodore Roosevelt came up time and time again as glasses of amber fluid were passed over the glistening mahogany bar at the Point Hotel. The bar was always well patronized into the wee hours and many a good housewife who had left the picnic hours before rushed into the children's room to cover their ears lest they hear the raucous songs and words of the more delinquent travelers. Then, too, there was the inevitable "Brush" when horsemen, moved by enthusiasm and alcohol, would match their trotters over the dusty highway. The clatter of horses' hooves, the shouts of the drivers as they urged on their steeds and the metallic whirring of the cart wheels echoed in the night until the sun made its first faint appearance in the sky.

Labor Day was always a big day at the Park and the Point. The story is still told that, on one of these holidays, a fire broke out in Valatie and only the late Chief Haddy and two more men were left in the village to battle the flames. The rest of the department was merrymaking at Kinderhook Lake. Today, both the Point Hotel and the Park are gone and only their memories remain for those who recall a time when life was more complacent and amusement was largely afforded by the simple and bucolic tastes of those who lived here a half century ago.

Time and a Half for Laboring on LABOR DAY

Right, as in overtime pay. That's what I'm supposed to collect for being here today, which is Labor Day, a full-fledged, God-fearing, constitutionally sanctioned holiday dedicated to those noble men and women who, by the sweat of their hairy armpits (the man, anyway) made this country what is today.

The fact that the country today is a mess is not their fault. Blame has yet to be assigned but that Man in the White House is always a possibility and has been for many a long underpaid year. Of course, I am not writing this on Labor Day and missing the BIG Chatham Fair. I have never missed a column deadline in 46 years, and I've never missed Labor Day at the fair except those years when my generation was fighting WWII.

If I were writing this on Labor Day I would be way past my Friday deadline and with any luck, it wouldn't appear at all, but editors aren't as tough as they used to be, and they like the occasional day off, too. So, he said with sickly supplicating smile, here we are, stuck with each other. Hi!

Its all quite confusing. The up-to-date thing among columnists—and, my, aren't there a lot of them—is to skip writing a column when the spirit moves them, or more precisely, doesn't move them. Thus, on some days, you pick up the old rag, turn to your favorite fount of wisdom and read that so-and-so "is taking the day off." If newspapers were accurate, which would certainly make them less entertaining, this sentence would read that so-and-so "has taken a day off"—which one, exactly, we may never know—and that's why his or her piece is not in place.

The line "The Black Hat Is Taking a Week Off"—has never appeared in this sterling journal. I don't say that proudly. In these enlightened times, this could mean I'm monomaniacal, driven, insecure, deadline-ridden and a good dancer. All these things are true, but the real reason is that I am from the old school. OK, make that Very Old School.

I was broken into "the game" to believe that the deadline was the holiest of holies, holier even than the Grateful Dead or the Republican Party. "Miss a Deadline, Go to Jail" was inscribed on the bumper sticker of my mind, a well-tuned line, if I do say so myself. Do I hear a second?

One of my all-time favorite bumper stickers was "The Marquis de Sade was A Young Whippersnapper." The young whippersnappers who are granted columns today think nothing of missing deadlines, sadistically or otherwise. It isn't part of their work ethic, or perhaps they weren't reared properly, a reflection of their "family values."

The irreducible minimum, I suppose, is my schedule of one column a week. I know a young whippersnapper who decided to take that day off. He thought it was a funny idea. Got away with it, too.

I'm not saying I have taken a lot of days off, but I write a column anyway because I'm a creature of habit. Veteran readers say chidingly that "I can always tell when you did write 'The Hat,'" as though I had a large staff of bad writers who can turn out the column when this even worse writer isn't in the mood.

Seriously, dear friends, hack writers like us are not allowed to have moods. It's not in the job description. At deadline time, it's "don't get it right, get it written," as the boozy old reporters used to say. As I near the twilight of a lackluster career, I can say without dissembling more than usual that I am proud to be a columnist, no matter what my batting average. He's a tough old guy who can play hurt and put out 100 percent every week of the year." Yeah, but 100 percent of what?

Well, er, 100 percent of stuff to fill the space all the way down to the bottom of the page. Sure, I make errors because I'm a feisty old guy who goes after every ball. Like fertilizer, I cover a lot of ground. Sure, I may be one step slower but (that's enough baseball metaphors—Ed.)

It used to be that becoming a columnist meant you'd reached the pinochle of success in this poker game. You become one the hard way, starting as a copy boy (now known as a copy person or "associate") graduating to cub reporter, doing a stint on the copy desk (to this day I admire a well-turned headline almost more than anything in the paper), covering the police beat, village town and county meetings, feature stories and so on. Finally, when they didn't know what else to do with you, they gave you a column or fired you.

"Kid's got a certain style."

"Yeah, but he makes a lot of mistakes."

"That's what I mean."

Well, I don't know why Labor Day turned into true confessions day, but a lot of kids who are now earning a living in the Fourth Estate owe their jobs to me. I've had them come in from journalism schools and they couldn't spell C-A-T.

Yeah, me. THE HAT, his finger flying over the keyboard of his beloved Loyal Royal. You can't call for copy paper from copy boys who never heard of copy paper, never saw a carbon copy and never smelled a printer's ink. I said "finger" because I still type with my right index finer and two on the left hand and turn out sloppy copy.

Once upon a time there were no columnists in this newspaper. In later years the publisher said, "I'm loading this paper with columnists and if one leaves, who'll care?"

That's why the *Courier* was eventually described as having "more columns than a Greek temple." Some of them are quite terrific and some aren't.

If you're still with me I trust yours was a Happy Labor Day. I used to put the knock on this holiday as sounding not very festive, but it's better than no holiday at all. And I had a great time at the BIG Chatham Fair, with my grandson—and that's the best way to see the fair, through the eyes of a child.

"It was the first innings that Coyote Leggett was presented first base on balls. Wabbly Wilder wagged his biffstick up against the ball for a sacrifice. Palmer cruised to first on extinct curves. Never More Decker, eager to shatter anything he could, came up."

"There was a reverberating roar and the ball whistled away through the air. Heliogabulus Howes and the ball met and stuck together like two lone girls when a tramp is trying to break through the back door . . . "

The literature quoted above is from an 1893 *Chatham Courier* describing a baseball game between Spencertown and Ghent, played at the Chatham Fair. Best of all were, and are, the nicknames—and there are no better nicknames to be found than in baseball. If you doubt it, consult the *Baseball Encyclopedia*.

There are zoological names—Frank (Dodo) Bird; Comments on the player's competence: Tim (Good Eye) Simmick; Names internally logical: Buck (Leaky) Faucet. For sounds alone: Bill (Goober) Zuber. Names invented by sportswriters with six months of college: Kent (Buy A Vowel) Hrbek. Those were players of yesteryear and today's nicknames, for the most part, are pallid and pathetic. I do like Doug (Eyechart) Gwosdz of Seattle, Mark (Amazing) Grace of the Cubs and Dennis (Oil Can) Boyd. Then there's Orel Hershiser, a real name that sounds like a German dentifrice.

But I hark back to that game of 1893 and can almost hear the chant that echoed over the fairgrounds—"Way to go, Heliogabulus, way to go!" Heliogabulus Howes was pitching but Ghent got to him for 14 runs in the 7th and there went the old ball game. Sorry, Helio.

⋙◦⋘

'The Christmas Village' . . . and hope eternal

Merry Christmas from "The Christmas Village." A merry charisma is a nice thing to have, too, this wonderful time of the year. We well recall some 60 years back when Chatham's one-man police force, Harry (Babe) Mack, who, when he was not enforcing the law, strung a few lights in what was then known as Bank Square—the site of the present village war memorial. Each year, Chief Mack added more and more lights and his efforts were augmented by the entire community. Houses and business places were festooned with lights and one year, the words "MERRY CHRISTMAS FROM THE CHRISTMAS VILLAGE" were spelled out on the side of the Masonic Building facing Depot Square.

Chatham's churches combined their choirs for a holiday chorale which also had a venturesome touch, as Henry ("Colonel") Alvord, a cherubic village pharmacist, would, attired as an angel, ascend to the village clock tower where, with the aid of a 1930s sound system, he sang "Adeste Fideles."

Chatham's reputation as the beautifully lighted "Christmas Village" became so great that on many occasions in the pre-World War II years, trains on the Boston and Albany would slow down so passengers could enjoy the sight of a community decorated brightly, but in good taste, for the Yuletide season.

As young persons, we thought Chatham's holiday decor could never be surpassed, but each year it has improved, and again this year, the great Christmas wreaths that adorn the village's business section are most attractive and Main Street stores are ablaze with displays that must certainly please "Babe" Mack.

Yes, it's Christmastide. Church bells ring and sinners pray mightily for a fast pass through the pearly gates. As the old wheeze goes, an old fellow from Spencertown's beautiful Punsit Valley arrives at the pearly gates and St. Peter sighs, "Yes, this is heaven, but you won't like it." It's a merry Christmas morning. The presents have been unwrapped and half of them are already broken. The other half can't be assembled by the old dumb fumbler and anyway the batteries are dead.

Old scene I remember from Chatham school daze. My French class teacher Irene Magee, holding up a book and saying, "Book is masculine." Familiar voice in class, "Of course, it's a hymn book." Hymns and hers are playing on the phonograph (that dates me). Or the hi-fi, the stereo. Stereo? One tries to keep up, I gave an LP— that's long-playing phonograph record with a hole in the middle— to my young friend, Lincoln Corsey, who said, "Gee, I'm not sure there's a turntable in our house, but I'll look around." I keep forgetting. Everything's a tape or a CD. Personally, I don't think a CD is that much better than an LP, unless you mean a certificate of deposit.

Christmas Day is long, joyous and usually cold. Chestnuts toasting on an open fire and all that. Overrated: roasting chestnuts. The permanent anomaly: The infant Jesus was born in the desert, but the classical weather is snow-ho-ho, besides which Santa is German. Even if he isn't, he looks German. Remember, he knows when you've been bad or good, and that is very German. My sainted mother, whose parents came from Alsace, sang Christmas carols in German. I was generally bad. Not only was she a sweet singer, she had a sweet swing, but I was a little shifty-footed.

What else is schmooze: one of my best holiday items in the 46 years I have been pecking out this column, was about the six-year-old boy in St. Paul's Church in Kinderhook, who didn't want to play the innkeeper in the Christmas play because he hated the idea of saying "No room at the inn" to Mary and Joseph. He finally agreed, but when he came to that fateful line during the performance, he blurted out, "There is no room at the inn—but what the heck, come in anyway and have a drink."

Christmas is the only holiday that's a season. Thanksgiving comes and goes in a few hours and except for the leftovers and the dyspepsia, can be forgotten until next year.

Christmas, however, is the whole enchilada. It starts just after Labor Day and by Thanksgiving, the tinsel is already beginning to look tired. Then it's time to lug the decorations out of the basement, find a tree that costs more than a mink, string the lights and have another toddy. Christmas can last as long as three months and ends in a stack of bills for items your friends and family have already returned. If you can get through the season without once hearing, "The Little Drummer Boy," you've won the game.

"Jingle Bells" holds up because it can be jazzed and swung and played every inch of the way. "Joy to the World" has the proper exultant tone. We need that and "Come All Ye Faithful" to remind us there is something to be celebrated that lasted 2000 years against all odds and oddballs.

Christmas is a delightful mishmash of fables, legends, traditions and geographical conundrums. This year the star shining in the east casts its glow over thousands of American troops on duty in Somalia—troops who came to feed the shrunken Somalian bellies, only to be shot, tortured, killed and dragged through the streets by those they came to feed—acts that mock the beneficence of Christianity and Judaism.

Here at home we search for the eternal simplicities: good and evil, sad and glad, beautiful and beastly. We try to unclutter our minds and psyches and return to the innocence of childhood when we thought we could make a difference and even shed light in dark corners. If Christmas can do all that, and it can, it is worth the effort. I marvel at the trouble people go to, the energy and money expended in the name of spreading holiday cheer.

Riding through the countryside in the gathering winter darkness and seeing a string of lights in the window of a distant farmhouse—a touch that makes you choke up a little.

Then there's the unbounded generosity of anonymous people who feed the helpless and clothe the homeless and lug turkeys to the free food places and work in the soup kitchens—all without the recognition they don't want or need. Tonight they can turn out their lights and read the newspaper by the light of their halos.

You have to believe that somebody is keeping score and putting high marks next to their names. If you don't believe that, the game is up and the party's over. He knows when you've been naughty, He knows when you've been nice, is it not so, Sire? And so, Merry Christmas, dear readers. The air is crisp, the vistas endless and hope eternal.

ACKNOWLEDGEMENTS

No book is ever the work of one person, and so it is with deep gratitude that I acknowledge the patient persuasion of David Forer, who fanned the embers to transform my columns into book form; to Mimi Forer, who created a design in perfect harmony with the material in these pages; to Nathalie Favre-Gilly, whose thoughtful editing and diligent marshaling of far-flung collaborators put the book on the road; to the late Baldy McCowan, for the original sketch that has graced the "Black Hat" column all these years; to David Forer, *père,* whose graceful and distinctive drawings brighten these pages; to Pam Cohen, who championed this effort with her legendary energy and enthusiasm; to Scott Wood, who became a warm and helpful colleague in proficiently representing the Crellin-Morris Association; to the Beulah Land Foundation for its generous support of this project; and finally to the Johnson Newspaper Corp. for allowing me to continue my weekly post-retirement offerings, until I have become the oldest living columnist in the world.

—A.S.C.